This Is My Story

75 Years of Miracles & Ministry

*This is my story. This is my song,
praising my Savior, all the day long.*

**Stories that will touch your heart
and inspire your faith in the living God.**

Rev. Richard W. LaFountain

Published by
Parousia Press
Grove City, Pennsylvania
www.PrayerToday.org
Printed in the U.S.A.

SECOND EDITION
REVISED AND CORRECTED
9/21/2022

ISBN: 978-0-9858879-6-4

© Copyright 2022 Richard W. LaFountain
All rights reserved.

No part of this publication may be reproduced, stored in a retrieval system, or transmitted in any form or by any means—electronic, mechanical, photocopy, recording, or any other—except for brief quotations in printed reviews, without the prior written permission of the publisher. All rights reserved.

All Scripture quotations, unless otherwise noted, are from the King James Version of the Bible or are the author's own translation or paraphrase. Other Scripture portions are from the New International Version.

In Dedication

I want to dedicate this book to my wife of 53 Years, Marilyn Ruth Smith LaFountain, who has stood by me and endured the telling of these stories in my preaching along with a hundred other anecdotes of our family life. And I dedicate it to our children, Aimee, who is in heaven, and Andrew and Angelica with their spouses and children. May the memories of God's mighty work among us never fade.

Index

Part 1 – God Who Calls Me

Chapter 1: My Family

Chapter 2: My Childhood Struggles

Chapter 3: My Faults & Failures

Chapter 4: My Encounters with God

Chapter 5: My Covenants with God

Chapter 6: My Crisis with God

Part 2 – God Who Helps Me

Chapter 7: God's Protections

Chapter 8: God's Providences

Chapter 9: God's Provisions

Chapter 10: God's Healings

Part 3 – God Who Equips Me

Chapter 11: God's Authority (Brazil)

Chapter 12: God's Deliverance (USA)

Chapter 13: God's Voice

Chapter 14: God's Anointings

Chapter 15: God's Restorations

Preface

I am not so egocentric as to think that everyone, or even anyone, would want to read about my life. I am not writing because I want readers. I am writing these memories for the generations to come. The hand of God has been active all through my life and I want my children, grandchildren and great grandchildren to know what God has done in my life so they will be encouraged to seek Him for His blessing and presence in their lives.

In my preaching I have often referred to events in my life to illustrate spiritual truths. People have responded to my stories saying, "You ought to write these stories down." As I age I am aware that with time passing I tend to forget things that have happened, or even to discard them on the trash heap of insignificant daily events.

I suppose it is not possible to relate all the significant stories and events of my life but I want to share those remembrances before they fade away. My dad had Alzheimer's during the last five years of his life. I pray that will not repeat itself in me, but having that disease in the family reminds me that now is the time to leave these recollections in writing so they might benefit someone who might encounter them.

One Scripture that comes to mind helps me know that writing my story is not in vain. It is Psalm 71:15-18

> *15 My mouth will tell of your righteous deeds,*
> *of your saving acts all day long—*
> *though I know not how to relate them all.*
> *16 I will come and proclaim your mighty acts, Sovereign Lord;*
> *I will proclaim your righteous deeds, yours alone.*
> *17 Since my youth, God, you have taught me,*
> *and to this day I declare your marvelous deeds.*
> *18 Even when I am old and gray,*
> *do not forsake me, my God,*
> *till I declare your power to the next generation,*
> *your mighty acts to all who are to come.*

Two factors have inspired me to write these memoirs: 1) I have been blessed and inspired over the years by Richard Harvey's *70 Years of Miracles*, in which he tells some of the stories of God's work in his life and 2) In 2014 while my mother was in a nursing home I realized that when she was gone it would be too late to praise her for what she had done to equip me for life. I took the opportunity to write a short tribute to my mother's influence in my life titled *I Remember Mama*. That short Mother's Day tribute was circulated in the nursing home and brought many to tears as they read the life history of my mother and her impact on my life. Now I want to expand that story to include the events and situations in my life that might be a help to others.

Rick Warren began his book *The Purpose Driven Life* with these words, "It's not about you!" As I sit down to write my memoirs, (for that is what these stories are, my memories) I am very aware that it is not about me. It is about the Lord and His work in my life. I take no credit for the great things He has done over the last seventy-five years. It is all God's doing, not mine.

I want to borrow some thoughts from Richard Harvey's great book, 70 Years of Miracles, concerning memories.

> "Some may ask, 'Haven't you colored it some?' I would answer that every true picture has its color and every person seeing or experiencing a scene in his life will describe it as he sees or remembers it. The coloring and tinting of it will be according to his own background, but still it can be all true. That is why the Gospels of the New Testament are all different, but not contradictory."

The stories I am about to write are my stories, the way I saw it, felt it, and remembered it. Others may have viewed it from different circumstances and would tell them a bit differently, but we are still all eyewitnesses of God's glory.

I am writing this book for my children, who might have taken part in some of these stories and who may have long forgotten them. I am writing these stories for my grandchildren who often have said, "Pop-pop, tell us a story." When I would begin telling them some make believe story they would hastily add, "No, Pop-pop, tell stories about your life." I am also writing these stories for my great and great-great grandchildren who just might run across this book a hundred years from now in some dusty old attic. They too must hear of the work of the Lord.

I am writing these stories for the hundreds, yes, thousands, of Americans and Brazilians who have heard me use these real life stories in sermons and who said, "You ought to write these down in a book."

So, here goes. This is my story. This is the story of my God and Savior Jesus Christ and what He has done in my life. His fingerprints are all over me, and I assure you there's more. I am sure I have failed to remember all the work that He has graciously done in my lifetime.

I want to assure my children and my children's children that Jesus is *"the same yesterday, today and forever."* What He has done for me, He will do for you when you call on His name. *"It is no secret what God can do. What He's done for others, He'll do for you."*

It is not an easy thing to write one's history for others to read. I'm no hero. I don't even consider myself to be special or in some way successful. I'm just me. As I write these stories it is not an attempt to appear to be something I am not. I will share my blemishes as well as my blessings, but in all that I write may Jesus Christ be glorified and praised. Just as the saints before the throne of God in Revelation 4:10-11 took their crowns and threw them at the feet of Jesus, so I take off any crown on my head and throw it down at the feet of Jesus and declare with all saints, *"You are worthy, our Lord and God, to receive glory and honor and power, for you created all things, and by your will they were created and have their being."*

To God Be the Glory Great Things He Has Done!

Part 1

In the Beginning

"Before I formed you in the womb I knew you, before you were born I set you apart; I appointed you as a prophet to the nations."
Jeremiah 1:5

Chapter 1

My Family

"His name is the Lord. A father to the fatherless, a defender of widows, is God in his holy dwelling. God sets the lonely in families, he leads out the prisoners with singing;" – Psalm 68:4-6

Meet My Family

Psalm 127
Children are indeed a heritage from the LORD, and the fruit of the womb is His reward. Like arrows in the hand of a warrior, so are children born in one's youth. Blessed is the man whose quiver is full of them.

<u>Mom</u> was the stable spiritual influence on each of us. She held the troop together. She had to bind up our wounds, and more often than not, to pray us through sicknesses, accidents, and the crises of life. Mom was the prayer warrior sitting in her favorite rocking chair every morning with her Bible and prayer list as she interceded on our behalf. Mom grew up in a non-Christian home with a lot of dysfunction. I didn't realize how bad it was until late in her life my mom told frightening stories of her home life. We are so glad that mom did not drag those dysfunctions into her home. God knows we all had enough dysfunction of our own. I thank God over and over that mom came to know Jesus as her Savior and brought us up in the nurture and admonition of the Lord.

<u>Dad</u> was the hard working absentee father much of the time. Mostly I remember dad sitting in his chair behind a newspaper. He read it every day, cover to cover. Dad came to know the Lord early in my life. I have vague memories of dad carrying cigarettes rolled up in his t-shirt sleeves. He would go to church with mom but would get out quickly for a smoke with some of the other smokers outside the church. I remember the day dad got saved. He had hightailed it out of the church as soon as the last verse of the closing song was sung. The pastor pursued dad outside the church and asked him if he didn't think it was time to ask Christ into his life. Dad followed him back into the church and knelt at the altar to receive Christ.

In many ways my dad carried the scars of his previous life that often interfered with him showing affection. I never knew my dad to say, "I love you." He didn't know how. He was not a touchy-feely kind of person. Dad had an explosive temper. He was a Jekyll and Hyde father, alternating between spiritual on Sundays to a carnal angry man on weekdays. Dad would have been called a "son of thunder" as Jesus nicknamed James and John. He grew up in a large family and was probably happy to go to work each day to escape the chaos in our home.

My Siblings

I grew up in a family with six children. I was the third child born into this family. As I look back on those days growing up together I thank God that He put me in a good family with four brothers and a sister. We had a lot of fun, many adventures, frequent mishaps, hilarious events, and bad things we did. But we were a pretty happy lot, at least that is what our spouses and children think when we get together and start to reminisce. Our stories provide lots of laughter and we have often heard our children say, "You ought to write these stories down."

Norma, the eldest and our only sister was the know-it-all big sister. She had her own room, unlike the rest of us. We boys shared one room and later in our teens, two or three to a room. Norma was our big sister. We looked up to her vast sum of wisdom in our early years. She taught us how to play baseball and instructed us in the sciences. Once as we lay on the grass contemplating the skies my brother asked her where thunder came from. Norma responded, as any big sister would, that thunder was clouds bumping together. I remember that because my brother David's teacher asked his class if they knew what caused thunder. David quickly raised his hand and said, "I know! It's clouds bumping together!"

David was a year and ten days older than me. He was the loud mouth, talkative, "say-whatever-comes-into-your-head" big brother. I remember mom and dad asking him if he ever thought before he spoke. To me it seemed that whatever he was thinking came directly out of his mouth with no filter. Dave was held back a grade in school because of missing much of the year with pneumonia. Being only a year apart in age put me in the same grade as David, to his eternal chagrin.

Dick, that's me, the quiet, shy, quick tempered middle child, who always felt cheated. I wore hand-me downs from my bother David when he outgrew his clothes. My other siblings inherited my cast off clothes when I outgrew them, which wasn't often, because I was short and my clothes fit longer than normal.

Mike, the next in line, was the handsome cunning, sneaky cheat. He was two years younger than me. Mike didn't look like the rest of us. He had dark hair and a Roman nose. I say he was a cheat because he could trade almost anything for something better. One day he came home from school with a transistor radio, which back then was a big deal. When my parents asked where he got it he responded that he traded it for a fountain pen.

Tom was born a couple of years after Mike. He was the runt of the litter. He became the comedian and goofball brother. He says he developed his sense of humor because he was picked on by the bigger boys at school. One day they even held him by his ankles dangling perilously over the school staircase. His one defense was to joke about it and make everyone laugh. When Tommy was just about two years old I remember coming into the living room and seeing my dad holding him on his lap in the rocking chair. I clearly remember it because it stopped me in my tracks. I remember thinking I had never been held by my dad like that and it made me jealous.

Steve, being the youngest, was born out of time, maybe he was an accident. I remember being in the car when my dad picked him and mom up from the hospital. He was a scaly looking kid. It looked like his skin was peeling off. Steve became the spoiled brat of the brood. I'm sure we picked on him a lot so he had to develop defense mechanisms to survive in our tribe. As a teenager (the rest of us were out of the home by then) he would disconnect the odometer in dad's new Volkswagen Beetle and cruise around while dad was sleeping from working midnights. Dad got so frustrated at the poor gas mileage he was getting that he traded in the VW for another car. Only much later did he learn what Steve had done.

We were all different. Each came under the same household, same parents and disciplines but each of us uniquely different. I am sure each has their own flavor of memories of the events that I tell.

Norma **David** **Dick**

Mike **Tom** **Steve**

Dad Memories

Proverbs 23:24
*The father of a righteous child has great joy;
a man who fathers a wise son rejoices in him.*

My dad grew up in a large family. I think they had five boys and three girls. His dad was at one time a motorcycle cop during the roaring twenties. When I knew "*Pipi*" (French for grandpa), he was a chain smoking, lower middle class hunting, fishing, and trapping farmer. My memories of him were of our rare visits to dad's parents. Usually they were gathered around the kitchen table smoking, playing cards, and drinking beer. I can clearly see my Pipi leaning on the potbelly stove smoking his cigarettes while other family members played cards. All of these activities were sinful vices so we were scurried off to the living room to sit quietly as the old folks visited.

Dad in the Army
Dad was in the army in WWII as a corporal working alongside a pharmacist, who often told my dad he would have made an excellent chemist or pharmacist. Dad worked in a psych ward for men who had post traumatic stress disorder, or who went berserk when they got that inevitable "dear John" letter. Most notable to me was the story Dad told of a huge man who went ballistic on the medics in an uncontrollable rage. Dad took him out with one punch to the jaw that left the man unconscious. Dad was short, but tough.

Dad, the Hunter
My first memory of my dad was that he had a shotgun and would go hunting pheasants out in the back of our property on Keagan Road. I remember that mostly because my brother Dave got to go hunting one day with my dad, which made me mad because I wanted to go. My mom had insisted on him taking my older brother though I don't think dad was too keen on the idea. They weren't gone very long before they were back. Probably because Dave was a talker and that would have driven my dad to distraction. Soon after that my mom insisted on not having a shotgun in the house with little boys around.

The Wild Game Dinners
Regardless of dad giving up hunting I have memories of his family providing us with occasional treats of small game. I remember dad bringing home a brace of wild ducks or geese they bagged on a hunt. Dad would pluck the feathers and mom cleaned and prepared them for a meal. She did not enjoy that, especially since we had to be careful not to bite into the buckshot still in the birds. Then there were the occasional

fish we were given by my uncles. We kids hated fish. It made no sense to eat something that you had to pick bones out of your mouth to eat.

Muskrat and Turtle

One day dad brought home muskrat from his family's trappings. I am sure they meant well but muskrat tastes like mud. I think that only happened once and my mom said no more. Someone in dad's family caught a turtle so we were to eat turtle. My brother Dave had a fit about it and stated that he would never eat turtle. My mom then secretly made turtle soup, or perhaps it was a stew, and served it to us without David knowing what it was. He asked for second helpings saying how good it was. Then mom asked if he knew what he was eating. He said no, but it sure was good. She then revealed that it was turtle. I don't think Dave was hungry for seconds after that.

Killing Rabbits

Dad decided to raise rabbits. We had a crawl space under our house that served as an ideal pen for the rabbits. We would occasionally get to coax one out and play with it. Then came the day that dad said the rabbits were big and needed to be killed and eaten. Oh, we kids had fits. Why would you kill our rabbits and eat them? But dad insisted that this was why we raised the rabbits. He then took them up to the unfinished attic and proceeded to knock them unconscious with a big club. I remember. I saw him do it. We all cried and ran downstairs to tell mom what a horrible dad we had. None of us wanted to eat rabbit stew.

Killing Chickens

Later in our childhood dad brought home a couple of live chickens that we were going to kill and eat. I remember dad saying, "You all like to eat chicken. Where do you think that meat comes from?" We had a small fenced in yard and dad let the chickens run around in the yard until he caught one to wring its neck and dip it in boiling water to prepare it for plucking. We thought that was so cruel. Dad said, "Well I can cut off the head if you think wringing their necks is cruel." He had left one chicken for last. He caught it and this time he didn't tie its feet. He laid it on a stump and chopped off its head. To our amazement the chicken jumped up and ran around the yard without a head as blood squirted out everywhere. We screamed, "Daddy, he's still alive!" Dad said, "No, he's dead, he just doesn't know it yet." Sure enough, the chicken soon flopped over and died. Later in life, that became a good illustration of Jesus' victory over Satan through the cross. Satan's power is destroyed and his doom is sure. His head is cut off but he doesn't know his doom is sure.

Liver and Onions
By far the worst meal we had to endure as children was the loathsome liver. Liver didn't often make it to our table, but maybe a couple of times a year we had to endure it. It was a disgusting mass of bloody slime before mom cooked it, and it wasn't much better after she cooked it. Mom would fry the thing till it was dry as a bone and shriveled up. Maybe she wanted to be sure it was dead and bloodless. We gagged it down with threats that we were not allowed to leave the table until all on our plates was gone. We were thankful to be able to drown it in piles of catsup. (When we had a dog we would secretly feed her under the table.) The worst of our liver-detesting world was when another poor and equally large family in the church invited us to have Sunday dinner at their house. They lived in a converted chicken coop, of all places. Mom warned us to be on our best behavior and not to mention their house being a chicken coop. To our horror they were serving liver for dinner, and NO CATSUP! Mom threatened us all with the belt if we so much as made an ugly face during the meal. We got through it and had a wonderful time with our friends, but we will never forget that liver meal.

Dad's Temper
My dad had a temper. I inherited my dad's temper. I tell these stories not to blame or shame him but to illustrate where I got my temper. My grandfather probably had a bad temper too, and I know my great grandfather had an evil personality and a bad temper. Later in life my dad told the story of going to his maternal grandfather's funeral and hearing the priest put him in the deepest hell saying, "This was the most evil man I have ever known." Dad said that made him furious and influenced him not to want to return to church.

As I previously stated my dad was saved when I was young. I'm glad dad got saved. Perhaps that was the only thing that kept him from walking off on his family. Mom, for all her good traits, was a nag. Like too many women she didn't have enough sense to let a matter go. She would harp on it non-stop until dad would blow up. I think he learned that blowing up was the only thing that would stop her. From my earliest age I remember dad's temper being his defining feature. Dad would sometimes throw violent fits of rage. I think it was to keep mom in tow. I thank God that to my knowledge my dad never hit my mom or was physically abusive in any way. Yet, dad had that temper.

My dad had his ups and downs spiritually. There were periods when he hungered after God. He became our Sunday School Superintendent and an elder in the church. I remember he even preached when our pastor was absent. I remember the sermon title, "Are you a Thermostat or a Thermometer Christian?"

The tenderest moment in my dad's life was during one of those spiritually alive periods. He and the pastor had been talking about going to visit my grandfather who was not a believer. Dad wanted to lead his dad to Christ but didn't know how, so the pastor agreed to go with my dad to talk to him about Jesus. They made the appointment but something came up that week and they had to postpone the visit until the following week. Early that following week my grandfather had a massive heart attack and died. I remember it vividly. As we drove to visit my grandmother Dad was so overcome with grief that he could not see to drive. He had to pull to the side of the road and wept bitterly. I can still see him beating on the steering wheel and saying, "Oh, why, oh, why didn't we keep that visit. My dad is in hell today because I failed to lead him to Christ."

Dad's Work Ethic
Dad was a hard working man. When he came home from the war there weren't many jobs available because so many men had come back at the same time. I remember my dad saying he would go to the local paper factory every day and ask for work. Finally, when they began to hire dad was one of the first to be hired. The personnel manager told him he got hired because he proved he desperately wanted to work. Dad worked at Consolidated Paper Company the rest of his life, often working seven days a week, twelve hours a day, and at times pulling double shifts. Though my dad made good money while he worked, too often the company would go on strike and dad could be out of work for months. Other times they didn't have enough work and would lay people off. At those times dad would not be content to sit around pulling unemployment. He would work roofing jobs or whatever jobs that became available to bring us through.

Those were often tough times for my parents. In times of prosperity dad would buy a house, but within a couple of years layoffs and strikes would leave us penniless and they would have to sell the house. We moved quite a bit throughout my life. That was not easy on my parents and didn't make them very popular with us. Having to move from school district to school district, always being the new kids coming into classrooms, was upsetting to all of us.

Easter and Christmas
Mom and dad tried to give us the best. I remember always having Easter egg candies and squirreling them away in our pockets as we went to church. I can't ever remember a bad Christmas. Mom and dad would somehow find the money or credit to give us a good Christmas. I have fond memories of looking at the Sears catalog to pick out what toys we wanted for Christmas. We were to circle several items and put our names by it so mom and dad could keep straight who wanted what. Mom and dad decided it was too difficult to keep us in our beds until

Christmas morning, so we had the tradition of opening gifts on Christmas Eve. My parents did not believe in teaching us to believe in Santa Claus. They would send us up to our rooms as they put our presents under the tree and around the room. Most presents weren't wrapped since we would only tear into them and leave a mess. It was always thrilling to walk into the living room and see the gifts under the lighted Christmas tree.

Being Poor
What I remember most about growing up was being poor. There were times when we would have to go to school with worn out knees in our pants that mom had ironed or sewed on patches. I remember the soles of my shoes coming unglued and flopping as I would walk to and from school. Dad would dutifully glue our soles and put them under a leg of the kitchen table till morning and send us off to school or church only to have the glue come undone. We often wore hand-me-downs, either from older siblings or from used clothes from other church families. That was embarrassing because sometimes kids would recognize the used clothes we were wearing, and being kids, they would call attention to it having been theirs.

Saturday night was shoe shine night and religiously we were to lay out our shoes on newspapers and shine them with liquid black polish. I also remember having holes in the bottom of my shoes and having to stuff folded newspapers in them to keep from wearing out our sock through the gaping holes.

Mom Memories

Proverbs 23:22
*Listen to your father who gave you life,
and do not despise your mother when she is old.*

Discipline at home
My mom had her favorite verses while we were growing up. One was *"Spare the rod and spoil the child."* (Proverbs 13:24) We got lots of spankings. We deserved it. We were rowdy, mean, disobedient, and deserved much of it I'm sure. We were always jealous of other children who didn't get spanked or who got discipline through a smack on the hands with a ruler, or a paddling with the flat of mom or dad's hand on the bottom. We were not so lucky. Mom always prefaced our spankings with, "This hurts me more than it hurts you, but God said, *'Spare the rod and spoil the child,'* this is for your own good." I'm sure when we were little mom might have used the flat of her hand on our bottoms, but soon she graduated to a belt. When the belt elicited a stubborn, "You're not going to make me cry" response from us boys, she started to use an electric extension cord. (Not plugged in.) That hurt!!! In fact, it left welts and bruises. My parents were fortunate that our teachers never saw our legs and buttocks or they might have called child social services, if that even existed back then. Too often mom would hold the spanking of us boys for when dad came home from work after a 12 hour day. Dad never said, "This will hurt me more than it hurts you." No, he made sure that it hurt us. We learned to scream and beg while being spanked hoping for some mercy. It never worked.

One time while waiting upstairs for dad to come home we decided to pad our backsides with extra clothes and magazines to lessen the effect of the electric cord. It still hurt.

Mom the Spiritual Leader
Mom could be counted on to be up well before the rest of us sitting in her rocker with her Bible open and her prayer sheet in front of her.

My mom was the spiritual director of our family. Dad was often off working, so much of our upbringing fell to mother. My maternal grandmother was the first to get saved, soon after my mother and my aunt came to know the Lord too.

My parents took us to church as often as the doors were open. Really, if the church doors were open, we were there lined up in the third row from the front on the right side. That was our pew. We attended Sunday School, morning worship and Sunday evening services every Sunday, plus prayer meeting on Wednesday nights. Then we were also in church for every weeknight Missions Conference and any revival or deeper life conference, sometimes two weeks at a time.

Devotions
Mom also made a habit of having family devotions with all of us children. We weren't allowed to go off to play without first having Bible reading and prayer. As we grew older mom was sensitive to the reality that this was very boring for us. She began reading us stories from Christian children's books and missionary stories. That helped. Our favorite was Paul Hutchens's series titled, *The Adventures of the Sugar Creek Gang*. It was funny, neighborhood children would come to the door and press their noses against the screen door to ask if we could come out and play. We always embarrassingly had to say, "Not until we have had devotions." They would ask, "Devotions? What is that?" I'm sure we responded with something like, "You don't even want to know." Devotions had an effect on us. Most of us prayed to receive Christ as our personal Savior at a very young age.

Leading Friends to Jesus
I remember in our first house on Keagan Road I was in the first or second grade. My good friend, Floyd Davis, would come over almost every day to play with me in our sand mound in our backyard. I was always envious of him. We had our cheap plastic trucks while he had those heavy duty Tonka trucks with backhoes and front loaders. We'd play and sometimes the subject of going to church would come up. I would tell him about heaven and hell and that he needed to pray to receive Jesus into his heart. I remember asking him day after day if he had asked Jesus to come into his heart. He would say, "Oh, yah, I forgot. I'll do it tonight." One day when I asked him he burst into a big smile and said, "Yes, I did. I asked Jesus into my heart last night." I never knew if that conversion really stuck with him or not, but after my college days I returned home and I heard that Floyd became a minister in the Lutheran Church. I guess something stuck.

The Stereo Record Player
When we were in our young teen years mom must have been very frustrated trying to keep our attention at devotions. One day a door to door salesman stopped by selling a stereo record player console cabinet with a package of Gospel music and a series of audio stories by Ethel Barrett. It also contained the audio Bible (King James Version of course) and Clyde Narramore's *Psychology for Living*. I don't know how they managed to afford it or how she convinced my dad this was needed, but they bought the set, which proved to be invaluable in giving me a desire to be able to tell stories like Ethel Barrett.

Mom's Prayers
In the LaFountain family you couldn't get away from prayer and a consciousness that God's presence and watchful eye were about the place. If we were going off to school mom would often want to pray over us before we went out the door. If we were sick mom would pray, usually with a hand on our fevered heads, and rebuking the fever in Jesus' name she would commit us to God.

There were times when we were bad and deserved a good spanking that mom would first stop to lecture us on obedience and say she was praying for us. Sometimes she would take us aside for a one-on-one conference about our relationship to God and what our disobedience and rebellion would bring later in life. She'd always want us to pray too and ask God's forgiveness before getting that whipping. I don't remember that our prayers ever saved us from a good thrashing, but it certainly left an impression. There were occasions as we grew older that she would add that she expected a trip to the altar at church the next Sunday if we really were repentant.

Going To Church
Getting ready for church was a hoot. Can you imagine getting six children in various states of chaos dressed and ready for church on Sunday morning and that with only one bathroom? It was chaotic. There were many arguments and so much fighting going on you'd think fire would come from heaven to consume us. But a miracle happened every Sunday morning, as soon as the car doors opened to get out at church we were little angels and mom and dad were all smiles like nothing ever happened.

Our Church
We had the privilege of going to a church under the ministry of some great preachers. Rev. Swaney was one of my favorites. He preached with passion. I don't remember any messages but I remember him sweating as he preached his heart out. His shiny bald head would pour down sweat as he preached. We had great musicians in our church. Ira Bleyaert on the piano, my Uncle Gene the organ, Mrs. Dunbar on the xylophone, and a full drum set where normally you would see the communion table. There were trumpets, trombones, an accordion and harmonica to enhance our worship. This was all back in the 1950's during the time period of Rev. Don Swaney.

Shekinah Glory Came Down
I remember one church service in Monroe in which the Holy Spirit came down in awesome power on the congregation. They called it revival. I remember hearing Mom and Dad talking about it in the car on the way home. They mentioned the shimmering fog-like presence that appeared

on the platform. When they said that, I remember thinking back to the service and remembered seeing that fog above the preacher. In my childlike heart I said to myself, "Huh, so that's what that was!" I never forgot it. I have preached about the *Shekinah* glory and used that illustration. I later found out that Jack Hayford has seen the same thing in his church. Mom may not even remember that experience, but it impacted my life greatly with a hunger to see and experience that presence of God.

Children's Programs
We also had the benefit of a children's program called *Jet Cadets* that encouraged Bible memorization through prizes and awards. We also had some amazing leaders and Sunday School teachers that loved us and taught us well. Many of them followed us in our spiritual journeys on into adulthood. Of course as with most churches we had the few boring teachers that simply read the lesson, but for the most part our memories are positive despite the damp church basement with mildew and peeling walls.

I always enjoyed having men for teachers, not because they were better than women teachers, but because we needed heroic male role models. One of my favorites was Glen Wilkins, an ex-boxer with a cauliflower ear. He impressed us. Then there was one pretty young mother who was loving and kind but to whom the boys in our class were relentless in their godless challenges to the existence of God, just to get her upset. I will never forget the day she ran from the class in tears because she could not answer their questions.

Vacation Bible School
Vacation Bible School was always a special treat. It sometimes went on for two weeks. We didn't mind. There wasn't anything else to do with our summers. When we lived out in the country on Keagan Road we were encouraged to invite our friends and neighbors to bring them to VBS. Mom didn't drive and Dad was always at work, so we arranged with a farmer to pick us up with his old truck. We all sat in the back singing choruses during the 20-minute ride to church. I don't ever remember getting rained on and no one ever fell out either. Many of our friends came to Jesus because mom and dad were faithful to encourage us to get our friends to Vacation Bible School and church.

Chapter 2

My Childhood Struggles

"Before I formed you in the womb I knew you, before you were born I set you apart; I appointed you as a prophet to the nations."
Jeremiah 1:5

Boys Will Be Boys

Proverbs 20:11
*Even a child is known by his doings,
whether his work be pure, and whether it be right*

Cowboys Jumping
Mom certainly had her share of troubles and trials with her children. When David and I were very young we were playing cowboys and indians using our tricycle as a horse. We had seen a cowboy on TV jump onto his horse from behind and we thought that was quite clever. We climbed onto the shed with a sloping roof, known then as a coal bin, and launched ourselves tentatively onto our tricycle, which was our horse. Mom was at the window doing dishes and shouted for us to stop because we could get seriously hurt. Well, one last jump to get down couldn't do much harm. Dave jumped one last time, evidently with his tongue sticking out. When he landed he bit his tongue three quarters of the way off. It must have been a neighbor who rushed him to the hospital. The doctor sewed his tongue back on. Mom prayed. After a period of recovery Dave was able to talk again and has never stopped since.

The Rat-Tail Comb
During our childhood David and I shared the same bed. On one occasion we were to be taking a nap, but of course we weren't. I don't know what I was thinking, maybe there was wax in Dave's ear, I don't remember, but for some reason I stuck a rat-tailed comb into his ear perforating his eardrum. My brother's memory was that I was pretending the comb was a gun and pointed the barrel at him and perhaps he moved the wrong way, but the result was the same. His ear drum was damaged. Mom prayed. Dave can hear as well as any of us and Dick got a good spanking for that one. "What were you thinking?!"

A Smashed Finger
When I was about five years old I was playing outdoors and daydreaming, using my imagination, as I was often prone to do. It was a windy fall day and I was holding on to the door jam pretending I was on a ship sailing a windy sea. About that time my sister ran out the door. I remember hearing my mom yell, "Norma, close that door!" She did. What she didn't know was that my right pinky finger was in the doorjamb. What a horror flashed over me to find my finger smashed and stuck in the door jamb. I'm sure the whole neighborhood heard me scream. I still remember it as if it were yesterday. When they opened the door my pinky was smashed flat and dangling half off. They rushed me to the hospital with the blood from my finger soaking towels. The doctor took

me in and did surgery on my little finger. I remember they kept me a day or two. What helps me remember was as a middle child even at that age I got very little special attention. In the hospital they brought me presents. I felt special. My finger recovered just fine, except that it still looks deformed and doesn't grow the nail properly. I share that story, not for pity, but to show how much my mother had to endure with her six children and how she always prayed us through.

Kindergarten

When I started kindergarten we had just moved to a new house in the country which meant we had to take a bus to school. School buses are quite traumatizing for shy children. My first day of school was later than the rest of the class because we had moved in the early fall after school already started. I remember it well because I was embarrassed to be singled out to the whole class. My mother took me in and introduced me to my teacher. "This is Ricky LaFountain." That was my name, Ricky, as in Ricky Ricardo from the *I Love Lucy* show. When my mother finally slipped out of the room the teacher introduced me to the whole class as Dickie LaFountain. The name stuck and I was ever after Dick or Dickie, except when my mother was angry, then I was Richard William LaFountain.

Color Blind

Kindergarten is a fun time for most kids. It was fun to go to school and play with the other children learning new things. For me it was a traumatic time. I was terribly shy and never spoke up in school. I also was colorblind but nobody knew it back then. I didn't know it either. Other children would make fun of my purple sky and brown grass. It all looked the same to me. So, in the first grade, once I learned to read the colors, I would refuse to use any crayon that did not have its original wrapper on it identifying the color. It was my way of surviving.

Dog Bite

Early in the year I was waiting for the bus, standing by our mailbox while my mother watched from the window. As I waited a neighbor dog came by. He seemed friendly so I reached out my hand to pet him and he bit me! He really chomped into my hand too. Off to the doctor I had to go to get a tetanus shot. I hate tetanus shots, they hurt!

Our doctor was a woman, Dr. Ames. She was a nice chubby lady with gray hair. She had delivered me and knew our family well. She had dealt with my smashed finger, my dog bite, and all of our inoculations. Sitting in her waiting room was frightening. It smelled like antiseptics. Then when we would go into her office it smelled like alcohol. When the time came to give shots she would reach into what looked like a little refrigerator and pull out an aluminum tray with hypodermic needles in it.

We knew what was coming. Rarely was the shot administered in the arm. She preferred the buttocks. How embarrassing! She was a woman and we had to pull our pants down for her. After, she would give us a stick of *Wrigley's Spearmint Gum* as if that made it all better. To this day I cannot stand the smell of spearmint gum.

Think! Think! Think!
Being shy I never raised my hand in class, except to go to the bathroom, and I refused to indicate my toilet need with one or two fingers. That was nobody's business. I am sure I wasn't the brightest bulb in the class either. I probably had attention deficit disorder, but no one knew about in those days. I didn't like school because it put me in a social setting and I was very shy. I remember being so shy that when company would come over to our house, even if they were my cousins, I would hide in a closet or under the bed hoping they would go away. Much of my classroom time was spent in daydreaming. What a shock it was early in first grade to get one of our test papers back with a huge red X across the page. I hadn't followed the instruction to underline an answer. Instead I circled the answer. The teacher gave out my test last and in front of the whole class. She thumped my head with her finger and said, "Think! Think! Think!" – I hated school ever after. It was a place of humiliation.

Poison Ivy
We lived in the Keagan Road house in the country for a number of years. It was there that I had my first bout with poison ivy. Well, we thought it was poison ivy. Across the street was a huge field of corn. We would play hide and go seek in among the stalks. It was great fun. The day after playing in the corn I broke out with a rash. We thought it was poison ivy. It wasn't. It looked like poison ivy. It itched like poison ivy, but it was much worse.

First they treated it with Calamine Lotion. That was about like caking white mud on my rash. The rash would soon start to ooze a yellow puss. Then whatever the puss touched, the rash spread until it spread all over my body. It got so bad that I was hospitalized with it several summers. I was their guinea pig. They tried soaking me in a purple chemical bath. That didn't help. It got worse. Then they decided what I needed was Aveeno oatmeal baths. I smelled like a breakfast cereal, and it did no good either. These were the days before antihistamines and corticosteroid shots. They finally decided it was weed poisoning, not just poison ivy.

Year after year on into my teens I got this horrible rash that made me feel like a leper. I was covered head to toe with calamine lotion and oozing sores. It usually hit me about July when my parents had their two week vacation. They weren't about to stay home from vacation because of my poison ivy. So they would wrap my arms and legs with gauze to keep the pussy sores from running all over everyone. We would go camping in the northern part of Michigan. It certainly was no fun for me. I looked like Lazarus just coming out of his tomb. Kids on the playground would run away from me. I wanted to run away from me. I itched horribly from head to toe and in between my toes and on all my bodily parts. But I was told not to scratch it because that only spread it. I remember asking God why he allowed this horrible disease to afflict me. Sometimes at night I would pray to die. That's how bad it was.

As a teenager I continued to battle this weed poisoning every year. My mother knew I was hoping to be a missionary. She had asked God for that. Seeing my misery she asked if I was sure God called me to be a missionary. She said, "If God wants you to be a missionary He is going to have to heal you of this weed poisoning." The rest of the story I will relate in chapter eight.

Chapter 3

My Faults & Failures

Even a child is known by his doings, whether his acts are pure, and whether it is evil.
Proverbs 20:11

For all have sinned and come short of the glory of God,
Romans 3:23

My Faults, Sins, Failures

Proverbs 22:6
*Train up a child in the way he should go:
and when he is old, he will not depart from it.*

Just because God saves you and calls you it does not mean you are perfect and do not have struggles with sin. We all must battle with the old nature and this sin infected world that wants to bring us down. I'm not going to tell you all my sins, but let me illustrate a few childhood sins that afflicted me.

My Secret Sins

My mother saturated us with prayer and the word of God. Mom drilled into us her other favorite biblical quote: *"Be sure your sin will find you out."* (Numbers 32:23) We knew that we could never get away with anything that mom wouldn't know about later. How did she know? She would always warn us, "God tells me", and He always would.

Sometimes it was God who told her, but other times it was one of my brothers. Once when we lived in the town of Monroe, Michigan we lived a few blocks from the river where we took up fishing and hunting for crayfish under the bridges. One day we discovered an old waterlogged Playboy magazine with pictures of naked women on every page. The only time we would have had contact with something like that was in the forbidden basement of our grandfather who had nude calendars on the walls. Of course, in our curiosity we had to find out what was so bad down there. Once our mom found out about the calendars we were banished from descending to that pit of hell.

We couldn't believe our find! We had no knowledge of those things. We couldn't believe women looked like that underneath those clothes. This was way better than grandpa's basement calendar. So, rather than avoiding those images (curious minds want to know) we took that waterlogged magazine and hid it in a crack under the bridge where we could return to study it more thoroughly. We swore ourselves to secrecy with an ominous feeling that somehow mom would find out. She did.

One day we made the mistake of having a little brother along when we visited our palace of porn. When he spied what we were looking at he grabbed a page and ran all the way home to tell mom the news of what Dave and Dickie were doing down by the riverside. How embarrassing! I'm sure that lecture was a livid tongue lashing. Dad got dragged into the spanking phase of our punishment. (I overheard my dad say, "What did you expect, boys will be boys.") But what I remember most was not the lecture or the spanking, but the certainty that mom knew, or would know, everything we did. God talked to mom.

Toilet Paper Adventure

While we lived in town on Wadsworth Street we had only one bathroom and that without a window or fan. Mom and dad would often light a match to dispel the odors in the room. That was our cheap air freshener. One day I was sitting on the toilet and saw the matches sitting on the back of the toilet. I decided to play with them, lighting and dousing one after another. Soon that got a bit boring. I wondered if toilet paper would burn slowly or rapidly. I got my answer in a blaze of flame. It burns quickly! The whole roll seemed to catch fire. I quickly doused it with my hand but it left burn marks on the wall. I tried everything to clean those marks. I tried soap, Ajax and bleach. Nothing would remove those stains. Being clever, I decided to unroll a few sheets of toilet paper and left it dangling enough to cover the marks. Within the hour mom called everyone to line up in the kitchen. We were in trouble. Someone had played with matches in the bathroom. She found the marks on the wall (God told her). Now she wanted the guilty party to step forward and confess or all of us would get a spanking. There we stood, six little innocents all standing in a row. I was under great conviction and was about to step forward as I secretly prayed, "Lord, deliver us now and in the time of our death," when suddenly my sister, Norma Jean, burst into tears and confessed that she had played with the matches and left the burn marks on the wall. She got the spanking and I got off scot free. But I learned a lesson – *"Be sure your sin will find you out."*

That "sin" of hiding my guilt dogged me for many years until as an adult my siblings were remembering events of our childhood and the toilet paper episode came up. I finally admitted to my sister that she took my punishment and that I too had played with matches in the bathroom.

My Mean Streak

I was probably 9-10 years old when we had a streak of stolen property. Our ball gloves, baseball bats, baseballs, and a myriad of our precious possessions suddenly disappeared from our backyard. It didn't take us too long to figure out who was pilfering our treasures. It was a little boy who lived down the street. I could best describe him as a kleptomaniac. He had sticky fingers. Nothing was safe when he was around.

We were cartoon addicts in those days and cartoons weren't always the best examples of good behavior. I remember having seen Bluto in the Popeye cartoons doing a mean dastardly trick on a monkey that kept begging for money. In my mind I thought I would teach this little brat a lesson. I would lure him into my trap by offering him some easy money in the shape of a quarter. My plan was to heat it up, offering it to him just like Bluto did. I hoped he would take it and scald his hand which would teach him to never steal again. The day came when my parents were away. The little neighborhood thief came into our yard again. Being aware of his thieving hands I went into the kitchen, got the tongs, and proceeded to heat up a quarter on the gas stove. (Bluto did this to the monkey). I called him to the door and said, "Hey, Billy, you want some money?" Of course he eagerly said, "Yes!" and I threw him the hot quarter. He instantly grabbed it. There was no immediate reaction when he first grabbed it in his fist. Then his eyes got real wide and he screamed bloody murder and ran home still clutching the quarter.

I felt bad for his scalded hand. I thought the matter was done and he had learned his lesson, but when my parents got home the phone rang. It was his parents furious and threatening to call the police for such an act of terrorism. I don't remember how my parents got out of a lawsuit or an arrest but I did get the spanking of my life! I only remember my parents saying, "What were you thinking?!!" Obviously, I was not thinking clearly. I was thinking of doing unto him as he did to us. It was another lesson to show me that my heart was deceitful above all things and desperately wicked.

My Temper

I had a temper. I had a bad temper. I had an explosive temper. I had a violent temper. I had my dad's temper. My temper often got me into trouble.

I remember a particular time when I got into a knock down drag out fight with my brother Mike. He was younger than me, but we were about the same size. I was a runt and he was growing rapidly. We got in a fight out on our ball field. He managed to put me down on the ground in a headlock, which wasn't easy to do, and he wouldn't let me up. Then he added a Dutch rub. (A Dutch rub is when you take your knuckle and rub it into someone's hair.) I got madder and madder and said so, "Mike, when I get up I will kill you!" I meant it. I was furious! Then I warned him again, "Mike, don't you ever let me up, because when you do I'm going to kill you." He did let me up. When he did I went berserk. I jumped to my feet and with all my strength I clobbered him with a round-house fist right to the eye. I heard and felt a crack as he screamed in pain and dropped like a sack of potatoes.

Mom heard the scream, as did everyone else, and Mike was rushed to the hospital emergency room. Once the dust settled and it was determined that Mike would live, howbeit with a huge black eye (which later I was quite proud of having given him), Mom took me aside into her bedroom and had one of those sermonizing and deeply convicting talks. I remember that one because she was right. She said, "Dickie, you have your dad's temper. When you get mad you lose all control and if you don't get it under control some day <u>you</u> <u>will</u> <u>kill</u> <u>someone</u>." Then she suggested a trip to the altar for victory over my temper. I knew she was right. I had a bad temper and when it hit I would go crazy and lose control of myself. I went to my room that day feeling horrible. I had come very close to killing my brother. If I had laid my hands on a baseball bat I think I would have beaten him to death. That's how out of control I was.

I did go to the altar that Sunday to ask the Lord to forgive me, though secretly I was quite proud of the shiner I gave my brother. When the elders knelt to pray with me I began to cry and told them about my temper and that I could not control it. They prayed with, for and over me that day that God would remove that poisonous temper from me. And He did!

Chapter 4

My Encounters with God

*"Faithful is he that calls you,
who also will do it."*
1 Thessalonians 5:24

My Conversion Experience

John 3:7
Do not marvel that I said to you, 'You must be born again.'

My mother believed that we all had to come into a personal relationship with God through Jesus Christ. Each of us needed a personal experience of being born again. For me that day came when I was very young. I remember it clearly because it is the same day my brother Dave gave his heart to Jesus and he was seven years old. I was a year younger. We had been sitting at the kitchen table eating lunch in the first house we lived in on Keagan Road. We were eating tomato soup with saltine crackers and peanut butter. I think it must have been a Saturday. Mom was telling us about heaven and hell and the end of the world and that we needed to "get saved" or we'd go to hell. I didn't care. I was having fun with my friends and hell was a long way off. I remember clearly the hardness of my little heart. David said, "Mommy, I want Jesus as my Savior. I don't want to go to hell." Mom took David into the bedroom so he could get saved. Little Mike followed them into the room. I stayed behind.

My big sister Norma, alias, Jeannie, came back into the kitchen and continued to preach mom's sermon to the only heathen left at the table, me. She preached a hell fire and brimstone sermon. I remember it. I remember her saying, "All of us are going to heaven except you, Dickie. Don't you want to go to heaven when you die?" I clearly remember my answer was an emphatic, "No!" Then she really laid into me with the fires of hell. Finally, seeing she was getting nowhere, she added, "Besides I'm going to tell Mom what you said." That did it. I must have figured I would get a whipping to get heaven knocked into me and another hotter place out of me. So, I went into the bedroom. It is weird how some things stick in your memory. As I arrived in the bedroom David and mommy were crying and praying, so being a good imitator, even at that age, I started to imitate crying.

At the end of that mom turned to David and said something like, "David, what just happened? Did you ask Jesus into your heart?" Goody two-shoes David said, "Yes, mommy, I asked Jesus in to my heart and he came in and I am going to heaven." Then she turned to me and asked, "Dickie, did you ask Jesus into your heart to be your Savior?" It was like time stood still for a moment. I suddenly realized that I had not asked Jesus into my heart. I cried. I am sure I must have prayed something, but could not remember what. I panicked. If I said 'no' I would get a sermon or a spanking. If I said 'yes' I would be a liar and really go to hell. I did what any red blooded American boy would do, I lied. "Yes, mommy I asked Jesus into my heart too." Mom hugged and kissed everybody as though the whole world just got saved. With that they all traipsed back into the kitchen to finish lunch – all, except for me. I remember it all so clearly, like a film rolling in my mind.

I stopped in the hallway really under a heavy sense of conviction that I had lied to my mom and was now really a sinner and headed to hell. I paused, leaned against the wall on my right shoulder and said, with eyes half open half closed, "Jesus, I lied. I am a sinner. Forgive me and come into my heart and be my Savior. Amen." You see, I did not realize I was supposed to ask Jesus to come into my heart. I thought I just needed to go through the motions like my big brother and copy him. So I copied him. The revelation that I was a sinner and bound for hell came to a little six year old like a bolt of lightning. Don't tell me kids don't understand enough to get saved at an early age! They can. I did.

The back story to this incident is that when I was in college the leader of our gospel team had asked each of us to share our personal testimony of when we first came to Christ. I shared that I did not have a specific memory of the first time I asked Jesus to be my Savior. I must have responded and asked Jesus into my heart a hundred times for years during my childhood. He said, "Dick, there was a first time. Why don't you ask the Lord to bring that first experience back to your memory so you can nail it down?" That night I did so. I asked the Lord to reveal to me the very first time I opened my heart to the Lord. That night God gave me a dream, or better yet it was a memory, of the story I just shared with you. Even the smells and tastes came back to mind. Yes, I think it is very important that every child of God KNOWS when and where he first invited Christ into his life. God doesn't have any grandchildren. No one is grandfathered in because of growing up in a Christian home or church. Jesus said, "YOU must be born again." That new life happens when you ask Jesus into your heart and life.

My Call to Be a Missionary

Jeremiah 1:5
Before I formed you in the womb I knew you, before you were born I set you apart; I appointed you as a prophet to the nations.

Each of mom's children were taken to church and dedicated to God in a formal baby dedication. I wasn't aware of my dedication since I was still a very tiny baby, but I grew up with the constant reminder that Mom had dedicated me to the Lord. She told me that the Sunday after I was born on September 14, 1947, I was in the back pew of the church being nursed by her and by the Word of God.

In my case mom had prayed that God would make me a missionary. Thirty years later Mom's prayer was answered. Mom always made sure we all knew exactly what she prayed for us. I grew up with that awareness from my earliest memories.

As I've already shared, we had a big family and we were often poor. Our houses were small and our furniture was used and well abused. Yet Mom considered it important to expose her children to missionaries whenever possible. Mom was a missionary prayer warrior. So, when the week-long missionary convention came around every year Mom made it her business to invite the missionary over for dinner. What better way to expose her children to the exciting life of a missionary? With so many other families better off and with fewer children it must have seemed strange to the pastor to send a missionary to one of the poorest families in the church. Those missionary conventions and missionary visits had a profound impact on my life.

When I was nine years old I remember going to the altar at the end of a missionary service and dedicating my life to the Lord to be a missionary. If I remember right, he was a missionary from West Africa. I was stirred by the adventure of living in the jungle. I am sure in my innocence I thought it was more like being Tarzan than evangelizing, but God used that to mark me for life.

By the time I was in high school we were still going to those week-long missionary conventions even on school nights when we had homework and better things to do. In many ways we hated being dragged off to church every night, but the long term effect was to infect us with a love for God and missions. Though I wandered far from that call on my life, it still was stuck in my heart and mind.

A Bright New Hope

Jeremiah 29:11
"For I know the plans I have for you," declares the LORD, "plans to prosper you and not to harm you, plans to give you hope and a future."

I hated school. I loved study and learning but classrooms did not fit my learning style. Being ADD (attention deficit disorder) with a busy mind and loads of imagination much of my grade school years were wasted on daydreams, paper airplanes, spit wads, straight pin darts, and anything but listening to a teacher drone on and on. I really identify with Charles Schultz's comic strip, *Peanuts*. He depicts Charlie Brown's teacher with the sound of a trombone going, "Wah-wah, wah-wah, wah." That's about all I heard my teachers saying.

A fascinating thing happened in the sixth grade at Boyd elementary school. For the first time in my life I had a male teacher. That was rare. I believe it was God's doing. Mr. McNew also attended our church. I remember one day while I was doodling pencil drawings, making spit wads, and basically ignoring the teacher, that all of sudden Mr. McNew threw a piece of chalk at me as he was lecturing. I saw it coming. I ducked and it missed me, but I got the point. I was supposed to be listening.

That year he announced that we were to have IQ testing. I dreaded that. I hated tests, and still do today. I freeze on exams. I remember taking the test and thinking this was pretty easy. It wasn't asking a myriad of questions about science, math or English. It was different. It was more of a reasoning and logic test. It didn't really feel like a test. It was more of an exercise. It was one of the original multiple choice tests where you answer by blacking in a circle with a special pencil. That was easy.

The surprise came weeks later when the results of the IQ tests came back. Mr. McNew announced that he was astounded by the results, and though he was not supposed to reveal students' IQ, he said he thought it was important to do so for someone's sake in that classroom. So, he proceeded to list the top three IQ scores in our class of 30. Top dog was John Campbell. Everyone knew he was the smartest kid in the class with straight A's. Then, Trula Brooks, who was our neighbor and later became my girlfriend. Finally the teacher said, "And now here is the surprise. The third smartest kid in this class is...Richard LaFountain, and he gave the IQ score. I was shocked. My friends were shocked. The whole class gasped audibly.

Mr. McNew asked me to stay after class to talk with him. I was terrified. He said, "Dick, I don't know if you understand what this score means. With a score like this you could be anything you want to be, even the President of the United States. You have the potential to be anything you set your mind to be and have any career you choose." Then he said he believed something was hindering me from achieving that potential and it had to do with my home life.

He made a special appointment with my parents to come in and talk to him. That night he showed them my IQ score and compared it to my D and C classroom work. He was very honest and blunt with them. Later they told me what he said. He believed that there was too much criticism and too little affirmation in our home. They needed to be aware of holding me back by not believing I could do anything I put my mind to do. He said Dick needed positive reinforcement, not more spankings, less criticism, and more love and understanding.

But God knew I needed a teacher to believe in me. Mr. McNew broke all the rules and I believe he played an important role in changing my life. Despite all of this encouragement and hope not much changed in my life. I can't remember there being any significant changes in our home. Things continued as they always had. I had very low self esteem. I really thought the IQ test was a fluke and somehow I guessed at the right answers. I continued to hate school, be an underachiever, and to feel insecure. I had an inferiority complex. In later years our pastor, a professional counselor, said, "All the LaFountain boys have inferiority complexes." Obviously God had a work to do in me.

My Re-Commitment to Christ

Romans 12:1-2
Therefore, I urge you, brothers and sisters, in view of God's mercy, to offer your bodies as a living sacrifice, holy and pleasing to God—this is your true and proper worship. ^{2} Do not conform to the pattern of this world, but be transformed by the renewing of your mind. Then you will be able to test and approve what God's will is—his good, pleasing and perfect will.

It was in the middle of my 11th grade year that the Lord again got a hold of my heart and affirmed my call to be a missionary. I went forward one night at another missionary conference with deep conviction about what God had said to me when I was nine years old. I wept at the altar telling the Lord I was too shy and too stupid and too allergic to be a missionary, but if that was what He wanted I wanted to hear it directly from Him with no doubts. My grades were still the underachiever's D's and C's, and I wasn't a stranger to an F on my report card either. I did not have the grades to go to college. In fact, I was never sure I would pass to the next grade at the end of each year.

I was the shiest child in our family. I couldn't speak in public. I was a poor reader. I didn't ever raise my hand in class for fear I'd be wrong, and someone would laugh at me. Every year I came down with the dreaded "weed poisoning." How could I ever become a missionary?

I was not a prime candidate for missionary service. That night God got a hold of my heart and again called me to be a missionary. I told Him I couldn't and that I thought He had the wrong man, but God's Spirit persisted. That night, in the quiet of my upstairs room, when my brother Dave, my inevitable sleeping partner, wasn't in the room, I got down on my knees again and argued with God about my potential to do what he asked of me. In desperation I asked for a sign from His Word. I knew that was a dangerous thing to do. But I was desperate.

I opened the Scriptures and immediately my eyes fell on the page like a spotlight was shining on it. *"Go into all the world and preach the Gospel to every creature."* (Mark 16:15) I rejoiced in sobbing tears, "Okay, God, then You have to do what I can't do. You have to give me intelligence and discipline to get good grades so I can get into college. You have to take away my shyness and you have to heal me of this weed poisoning." God answered that prayer almost immediately.

From that moment to high school graduation my grades went from D average to the honor roll. I remember my brother Dave having a fit when I came home with an honor roll report card. He said, "How'd you do that? You must be cheating. You're just as dumb as I am." Yeah Dave, you're right. I'm as dumb as a brick, but God can do anything with anyone who is surrendered fully to His will.

Chapter 5

My Covenants with God

1 If you fully obey the LORD your God and carefully follow all his commands I give you today, the LORD your God will set you high above all the nations on earth. 2 All these blessings will come upon you and accompany you if you obey the LORD your God: 3 You will be blessed in the city and blessed in the country. 4 The fruit of your womb will be blessed, and the crops of your land and the young of your livestock--the calves of your herds and the lambs of your flocks. 5 Your basket and your kneading trough will be blessed. 6 You will be blessed when you come in and blessed when you go out.

Deuteronomy 28:1-6

New Covenants With God

Exodus 20:8-10
Remember the Sabbath day, to keep it holy. Six days you shall labor, and do all your work, [10] but the seventh day is a Sabbath to the LORD your God. On it you shall not do any work

There was another secret to this transformation. It came from Scripture. God gave it to me as a promise when I rededicated my life to the Lord. It was this, *"Seek first the kingdom of God and His righteousness and all these things will be added unto you."* I took that to heart. The Lord was to be first thing every morning, to spend time alone with him. Thus, I started a life-long discipline of daily personal devotions of Bible reading and prayer every morning.

Another discipline came at this time as well. I felt a strong conviction that I should dedicate every Sunday to the Lord. After all, it is called the "Sabbath Rest" and "The Lord's Day." So, I took God at His word from Isaiah 58:13-14,

> *"If you keep your feet from breaking the Sabbath and from doing as you please on my holy day, if you call the Sabbath a delight and the LORD's holy day honorable, and if you honor it by not going your own way and not doing as you please or speaking idle words, then you will find your joy in the LORD, and I will cause you to ride on the heights of the land and to feast on the inheritance of your father Jacob."* The mouth of the LORD has spoken.

I took that to heart. I felt as if the Lord were saying this directly to me. I was to set apart the Lord's Day to be His day, and not my own. How was I to do that?

First, I had the habit of procrastinating doing my homework assignments until Sunday afternoon, then I would rush and cram to get it all done, sometimes until late at night. The Lord said, "No more. I don't want you to study on the Lord's Day. Get it done by Saturday night"

With that deep conviction I began this new discipline of no school work on Sundays. If there was any one thing I did to change my grades it was this. All my homework, reading and written assignments were to be done by Saturday night so the Lord's Day could be my Sabbath Rest. The result was my grades improved and my Sundays became a delight to the Lord.

The other delight was to find a friend at church who had a likeminded spirit. His name was Rex Jones. Because I had no homework to do on Sunday night Rex and I would attend the evening service and often we would end up talking after the service then walking home as we fellowshipped together. Those years were delightful and I always looked forward to Sundays as a day of rest. This also afforded me the opportunity to participate in nursing home ministries, which I never had done before. This discipline gradually included no playing baseball or football on the Lord's Day. I am not implying by this that for others to do so is sin, it is not. But for me *"He that knows to do good and does it not, is sin."* (James 4:17)

The Test of My Sunday Covenant

Isaiah 58:13-14,
If you keep your feet from breaking the Sabbath and from doing as you please on my holy day, if you call the Sabbath a delight and the LORD's holy day honorable, and if you honor it by not going your own way and not doing as you please or speaking idle words, then you will find your joy in the LORD,

Shortly after graduating high school I decided I would have to work a year to earn enough money for college. I got a job working at Chrysler Engine Plant in Trenton, Michigan where many of my friends and family also worked. They seemed to love working there. It was great pay and there were usually opportunities for overtime. On my first day in that huge engine plant I had to walk a half mile in a closed building to get to my assigned department, which happened to be the piston rods area. I was given my assignment of stamping a pedal that reamed out burrs on the rods as they came down the assembly line. It was a dreary, brainless, monotonous job in a noisy factory. I said to the Lord that day that if He hadn't called me to be a missionary I would never ever want to work in a factory.

I worked there in the fall and all went well. The money was great. I was able to buy my own car and pay it off. I was able to accumulate my savings for college. Then came the day we were informed that production was picking up and we would have to work on Saturdays. That was no problem and it paid time and a half. A month later they said we would be going to 12 hours a day 7 days per week. We would have to work Sundays. There was a rule at the factory that everyone was required to do overtime or be overlooked for any extra hours. When they came to me to ask me to work on Sunday I graciously refused telling them that my Sundays were the Lord's Day and by my spiritual covenant that day belonged to God. The foreman wasn't pleased. He reiterated that all employees were required to work overtime and Sunday was no exception. If they made exceptions then half the work force wouldn't want to work seven days a week. I told him that this was my commitment to God and I was fine doing all the overtime they could throw at me, but not on Sunday. I would work 12 hour shifts and even put in double shifts if necessary, but I would not work on Sunday. He said he would have to talk to his manager and the general manager. I remember the divisional foreman came to talk to me as well telling me that if I did not work Sundays then I would not be offered any overtime. I told him that was fine with me but Sundays were out, even if it meant losing my job. The next day the foreman came around giving overtime slips and said, "LaFountain, you are to work on Saturday, but you are exempt on Sunday." Wow! I was amazed and delighted.

Soon word got out that LaFountain didn't have to work on Sundays. Guys would come to me and ask what made me so special that I didn't have to work on Sunday. I told them of my commitment to God and said that I was sure if they made that commitment they wouldn't have to work on Sunday either. I remember another Christian guy looking at me for a long moment then he said, "Nah, I love the money too much to give that up." So it was that I was not required to work on Sunday though everyone else had to. God is good.

Keeping the Covenant in College

Ezekiel 20:19-20
I am the Lord your God; follow my decrees and be careful to keep my laws. Keep my Sabbaths holy, that they may be a sign between us. Then you will know that I am the Lord your God.

I have endeavored to keep that covenant with God through the years, even in college. I remember one occasion in college that I had been working a fulltime job and dedicating Friday night and Saturday to the Lord in evangelistic ministries. I worked in an inner city mission in New York City every weekend. This particular week had been difficult and I had many assignments due on Monday. I had worked hard to complete all my assignments on time, but there was a speech due for Dr. Lias's class on Monday morning and I wasn't ready. The professor had said that if you were called on to give a speech you must have it typed out and then given orally that day. Well, I didn't have that speech ready and it bothered me all weekend that I could not work on it because of ministry. Sunday was off limits for that kind of thing. I told the Lord this was not working well and I needed to study that Sunday. The Spirit of God convinced me to keep my covenant with God and not do homework on Sunday.

There was an unwritten rule at Nyack college that if a professor did not show up within the first ten minutes of class, the class would be dismissed. Yet, everyone knew that Dr. Lias never was late and never ever missed a class. I knew I was only half ready with that speech, so I prayed, "Lord, you know I have obeyed and put you first, and I am willing to get a zero on that speech if that is your will, but I ask you to do the impossible and make Dr. Lias late for class."

The class bell rang that Monday morning and Dr. Lias was not there. There was a buzz of excitement in the air. Would Dr. Lias be late? Five minutes went by, then six, seven and eight minutes passed. Some students went out to the parking lot to see if he was coming. He was not. Nine minutes passed. Would he come? Then at the ten minute mark the whole class cheered and began filing out. On our way down the hallway Dr. Lias showed up, but he was too late and class was dismissed. Evidently he had been held up due to a traffic accident. This is the only time in all the years of college that Dr Lias was late for a class. God had done it. By the way, two days later I was called on to give that speech as I would have been called on Monday, but this time I was ready. He gave me an A+ and even applauded everything about that speech. God is good.

Special Gifts From God

1 Corinthians 12:31 & 14:1
But earnestly desire the best gifts. Yet I show you a more excellent way. Follow the way of love and eagerly desire spiritual gifts, especially the gift of prophecy

One of the things that bothered me in my teens was that I had no spiritual gift from God. Other friends could sing, play instruments, speak in public, and demonstrated different levels of giftedness, some natural talents and others special gifts for serving God. I had none. This was not just my perception; this was the opinion of others.

I sought the help of spiritual leaders such as Sunday School teachers, pastors, my favorite aunt, and even my mother. They looked at me and tried to evaluate where they saw giftedness. They all failed to point out anything special about Dick LaFountain. My mother, bless her heart, searched for something I did well. Finally she quipped, "Well, you made a wonderful little bird house." (That bird house was crooked and fell apart.)

I began to pray about this. How was I to serve God when I had no talent or spiritual gift? My brother Dave had a beautiful bass voice and was highlighted in church and high school productions. I had no voice. In fact, it was my reality that I sang in monotone. I sat next to a friend in our church and we sang together making joyful noises, but it was hardly singing in tune. It was more of the droning of one or two notes, then falling silent as we attempted to reach those high notes.

A Dream Changed It All

One night before going to bed I told the Lord that I envied my brother's ability to sing and that if He would give me the gift of singing I would only use it for him. That night a wonderful thing happened. I dreamed of singing with a choir and for the first time in my life I could hear the different parts of the song. I heard melody and harmony. I had never been able to distinguish that before. I guess I was not only color blind, I was tone deaf.

Then I woke up. I went down to the kitchen for breakfast. Mom always had a Christian radio station playing music in the mornings. I was shocked I could hear the melody and harmony! I remember it was the golden voice of Solomon King who was singing. I could sing along with him and it didn't sound bad. Something happened in my brain, my ears, my voice, and my spirit. I could sing!

That changed everything. I started to enjoy singing at church. Listening to music took on a new dimension. It was like having no taste buds, then suddenly being able to taste the different flavors. I didn't join the choir or sing solos or duets like my brother, but I began to really enjoy praising God in song.

In fact, God began putting songs in my heart to sing to him. Almost every day of my life the Lord gives me songs to sing. My wife will attest to the fact that I wake up with a song in my heart that echoes from my lips. That was a new thing and that was a wonderful gift from God.

The Brooklyn Gospel Team

Zephaniah 3:17
The Lord your God is with you, the Mighty Warrior who saves. He will take great delight in you; in his love he will no longer rebuke you, but will rejoice over you with singing.

A few years later while attending college we were riding in a van returning from a ministry in Brooklyn, New York singing songs, hymns and choruses as we traveled. Suddenly the leader of the Brooklyn Gospel Team, a gifted musician, turned to me and said, "Dick you have a wonderful bass voice. You should join our ensemble. We are going to be traveling during Easter vacation and singing in churches every night."

I tried out with fear and trembling and they accepted me into the group. What was really shocking to me was that in one of our numbers they asked me to sing a solo. That was a first! God did a wonderful thing for me.

It was on that tour group where my wife, Marilyn, and I began to fall in love. She was in that musical group as well and our hearts melted and molded as we sang.

In our first pastorate people found out that we sang together and we were asked to be the special music for several revival services. I remember one song we sang while still in college titled *It's Not an Easy Road*. We were rehearsing the song when it occurred to me that it sounded like we were singing, *"It's Snot an Easy Road."* We burst out laughing and could hardly ever sing that song without laughing at our diction.

Revival Breaks Out

Psalm 96:1-2
Sing to the LORD a new song; sing to the LORD, all the earth. Sing to the LORD, praise his name; proclaim his salvation day after day.

Many years later as I served as a missionary in Brazil I traveled to Uruguay to preach a series of meetings in a large church on the border with Brazil. As I was about to stand up to preach God began tugging on my heart. I felt him whisper, "You gave your voice to me, now I want you to stand and sing a song." I was terrified. Here I was an American missionary speaking Portuguese to a Spanish speaking church and God wanted me to sing to them. I thought that was very odd and maybe it wasn't the Lord speaking at all, but as I pondered that inner voice the assurance came that it was indeed God speaking and I was to stand, not to preach but to sing a song.

But what do I sing? Immediately I was given the song in my heart. It was *"No One Ever Cared for Me Like Jesus."* The words are, *"I would love to tell you what I think of Jesus, since I found in him a friend so strong and true."* I stood to the microphone, not even knowing if I would start on the right note, opened my mouth and sang. It was beautiful, right on key.

As I sang I could see their eyes light up. They knew the song in Spanish and began to sing along. As we sang people started to weep and some came running to the altar. I don't remember that I even preached that night but a revival broke out in the midst of that church that was inexplicable, except God gave a monotone boy a gift beyond music, a gift of the Spirit that moves hearts toward God.

Other gifts of the Spirit would follow at different times in my life and ministry. Usually the gift would show up at unusual times and places when it was most needed and would surprise me. Now many years have gone by and I often hear people say, "Pastor Dick, your have been gifted by God in so many wonderful ways." When I hear that a smile comes to my face and a tear to my eye as I remember this was the boy who had no talent or gift. Praise God from whom all blessings flow!

Chapter 6

My Crisis with God

I beseech you therefore, brethren, by the mercies of God, that ye present your bodies a living sacrifice, holy, acceptable unto God, which is your reasonable service.
Romans 12:1

High School – A Weak Witness

Proverbs 29:25
The fear of man lays a snare, but whoever trusts in the Lord is safe.

During high school I attempted to witness for Christ, but I failed miserably. I was afraid of what people would think. At one point in high school a group of my friends were talking about some other young people in our church who were attending a prayer meeting before school. They had mentioned some things about them and were kind of critical of Christianity. Attempting to be bold I spoke up and said, "Hey I'm a Christian too." My friends turned to me and said, "What? No way. You're not a Christian. You do the same things we do, and you say the same things we say. You curse and swear just like we do."

I know for a fact that I didn't curse and swear and I know I didn't do all the bad things that they did. But as I hung around them they identified me with themselves. They didn't see any difference between my life and their lives. That was an eye-opener.

I often prayed about that and told the Lord He was going to have to grant me boldness because I didn't have it. I knew how to witness. I knew the Bible pretty well and had memorized whole chapters. I could explain what Christ did for us when he died on the cross, but I couldn't do what other people did. I was a spiritual coward.

My brother David was in my same grade in high school. He is so different from me. He is a talker. I am not. He loved to meet new people. I did not. He had no fear of carrying his Bible to school and to speak out as a witness for Christ. Me, I was terrified to carry a Bible to school. A Bible doesn't belong in school. It's not like I would read the Bible at school. It was hard enough just to read all my homework assignments.

The only time I remember carrying my Bible to school was on the occasion in salesmanship class we were to give a sales pitch for some product as a speech. I couldn't come up with a good product to pitch but I thought maybe I could attempt to sell the Bible. The day came for my speech and I stood up before the class and put on my salesman act and huckstered the Bible. I praised it as the best selling book in history. I showed the beautiful leather cover, its flexibility. I talked about the content and the number of stories. In fact, I claimed to the class that the Bible contained every story imaginable. Then I asked the class to suggest a story they thought might not be in the Bible. They did, but for every story they came up with I could show them a Bible story with that theme. The teacher, a former Baptist minister, loved the speech and gave me an A+ on it.

Yet, to carry the Bible was difficult for me. On several occasions I attempted to imitate my brother by carrying my Bible to school but I always hid it under other books on my way to school or shoved it in my locker lest someone should see it. I was a very private Christian.

After High School

Romans 1:16
*"I am ashamed of the Gospel of Christ
for it is the power of God unto salvation."*

I graduated at 17 years of age. Since my parents had no finances to send me to college I decided to work a year to save money for school. I worked at the Chrysler's engine plant in Trenton, Michigan. I worked the afternoon shift, from four o'clock until midnight. I worked many long hours. It was hot. It was hard work. Yet it was a refreshing time because I had all of my mornings to myself. From seven or eight in the morning when I would get up I would have the entire day until 3:30 when I drove to work.

I would spend an hour on my devotions of Bible study and prayer. My delight that summer was to go to a private lake to swim and lay in the sun getting tan. It was a nice inland lake. While getting a tan I got out my Bible to continue reading through the New Testament. I was spending time alone with God. I didn't have anybody with me, so those days were precious to me as God was speaking to me about things in my own heart and life.

It was during that time that my brother David was also working at Chrysler's and he was quite a witness. He was a guy that liked to talk all the time and he seemed to be bold telliing others about Christ. He even carried a Bible to work. I thought that was admirable. I wished I could do that. As God began to work in my heart on this issue the Lord told me He wanted me to just carry my Bible to work. That would be a start I thought. But I struggled with that. As we came to work at Chrysler's we had to pass through a gate where the guards would check our lunchboxes. I was afraid that they would find my Bible and would ask me why I was taking a Bible into work when I was supposed to be working, not reading the Bible. But my brother Dave carried his Bible without any trouble, so I really didn't have an excuse.

Just Carry Your Bible

Deuteronomy 17:18-19
He (the king) is to write for himself on a scroll a copy of this law, taken from that of the Levitical priests. It is to be with him, and he is to read it all the days of his life so that he may learn to revere the LORD his God and follow carefully all the words of this law and these decrees

The process began. I decided one day that I was going to carry my Bible. I got ready for work. I packed my lunchbox I thought if I put it in my lunchbox no one would see it. I put my large Bible into my lunchbox and I walked out to the car, put the lunchbox on my seat next to me. As I sat there I lost my courage. I put it back in the house. I was miserable all that night, because I knew it was such a little thing to carry my Bible to work. Every day I would go through the same routine, but each night I tried I got cold feet. I would pick up the lunchbox, take the Bible out and put it back in the house.

In Luke 9:26 Jesus said

> *"If you are ashamed of me and my words before this sinful and adulterous generation I will be ashamed of you before my Father in heaven and before the holy angels."*

That verse kept going through my head and bothered me. It bothered me that Christ might deny me before the Father in heaven.

Each day through that week I attempted to carry my Bible. I was under deep conviction. I needed to do this to break my pattern of fear. The process went on through five or six days. I would try to carry my Bible. I would put it into my lunchbox, get in the car and actually drive to work. Then I would sit in the parking lot praying God would give me courage. Then I'd fail. I would leave the Bible in the car and walk into work. All those nights I would feel guilty that I couldn't carry my Bible.

For most people that would not be big thing, but for me it was a huge thing. I was called to be a preacher, a missionary, and an evangelist, but I couldn't do it. I was too shy. I was afraid of people. I've never been a talker. It was always difficult for me to have conversations with strangers. I wouldn't know what to say if somebody asked me a question about the Bible.

One afternoon I was getting ready for work and I was determined. I was adamant. I'm going to carry my Bible. This time instead of carrying my big Bible I took a little New Testament, one of those little Gideon New Testaments. I put it into my lunchbox. All through my half hour drive to work I was praying and telling the Lord I was going to be bold. I was going to be strong. I was going to carry my Bible to work. I was even going to read it during my breaks and lunch time. I got to the factory and I sat in the parking lot. I prayed and I prayed. I asked the Lord for courage. Then boldly I put that Bible in my lunchbox and closed it up. I closed the door on the car, locked and marched toward the guard shack. I got within 30 feet of the guard shack, I got fearful again, turned around and went back to the car. I threw my Bible in and walked to work. I said, "Lord I just can't do this."

The Night I Got Sick

Psalm 119:71-72
It is good for me that I was afflicted, that I might learn your statutes. The law of your mouth is better to me than thousands of gold and silver.

The walk into the factory was a long one. I had to walk a half mile all the way back through the factory to get to my work area. When I got to my department the man who worked with me looked at me and said, "Hey Dick. You look terrible. Are you sick? What's the matter" I replied, "Oh nothing, it's just a headache and I have a sunburn." But I knew it was more than that. I was under deep conviction. I felt I had failed the Lord. I failed this test. I knew that I could not be a missionary. I could not be a pastor. I could not be an evangelist, because I was too cowardly.

All through that evening at work I felt a fever rising within me. My face was beet red, but I thought maybe it was because of the sunburn. I continued to work while the fever was raging inside me. I felt sick.

When I got to the house my dad happened to be sitting in the living room. He looked at me and said. "What's wrong with you? You look terrible. Are you okay?" I said I thought I was getting sick and had a fever. Dad went to the medicine cabinet, got the thermometer and put it in my mouth. I did have a temperature. It was 102°. I took some aspirin and went to bed. I struggled to sleep because I was still ashamed that I couldn't carry my Bible. In the morning the fever was still there. My mom took my temperature and it was 104°. They rushed me to the hospital. There was something desperately wrong.

A Strange Life-Threatening Disease

Psalm 119:67
Before I was afflicted I went astray, but now I keep your word.

The high fever continued for a week. They kept me in the hospital and started doing tests. My doctor came in after a couple days of testing and said, "Dick I don't know what you have. We know that you have mononucleosis, but there's something else going on here. We don't know what else you have. You have a disease that we can't identify."

During that long fever I broke out with a rash on my skin, mostly on my hands and on my feet. I lost all my tan. My skin began to peel off, or rather, scaled off. The doctor came in again and warned me. She said, "Dick, you have an enlarged spleen. It's very dangerous and you still have a high fever. I'm warning you, do not get out of bed. Do not disobey this warning." Then she told me of a young teen in our town who had mononucleosis and a similar fever. She did not obey the instructions to stay in bed and her spleen ruptured and she died.

I was quite frightened by this. Six days passed. My hands and feet had gotten calloused and thick like elephant's skin. There were blisters all over them. Then I began to lose my hair. I lost half my hair. It fell out on the bed. The doctors continued to do tests. She came in again and warned me about getting out of bed. I had some rare disease they could not diagnose.

As I lay in bed night after night I knew why I was there. I knew that I had this fever because I was under conviction that God wanted me to do something that I could not do. I laid in bed struggling with God over this issue of courage.

Then the Lord spoke to my heart one night and said, "Dick, you could die tonight. I could take you home to heaven tonight. Or you can live for me the way I've called you to. The choice is yours. Either you surrender to me completely with no reservation, or you will die of this disease."

My Bed Became an Altar

Philippians 2:27
Indeed he was sick, nearly unto death. but God had mercy on him, and not on him alone but also on me, that I should not have sorrow upon sorrow.

I laid in bed weeping. I was trying my best to be a witness for Him, but I was a failure. I asked God to please spare my life but argued that He made me this way. I told the Lord I was trying but I could not do what He was asking me to do. Then the Lord spoke and said, *"You're trying to do it in your own strength. You're trying to do it as Dick LaFountain would do it. I want you to do it in my strength. I've created you to be a missionary. I've given you a new heart. I've given you a new mind. I can give you the courage you lack, but you need to surrender everything to me unreservedly."*

I remember so clearly what was happening that night as I lay on my bed. I felt like I was on the edge of a precipice and I was going to live or I was going to die. Laying in bed with tears streaming down my face I lifted up my hands to heaven with those tears streaming down my face and said, "Oh Lord, I give you my all. I cannot do this. I give you my heart. I give you my mind. I give you my body. I surrender my soul to you Lord. I need you. Without you I can't do this, so I give up my rights. I give up my privileges. I give up my will. I surrender to you Lord. I want you to be Lord of all."

With that I finished my prayer and went to sleep. I don't know what happened but something changed. When I woke up in the morning they tested me again. The doctor said, "Your fever has broken. You are starting to mend."

I stayed another week in the hospital. The doctor came in after that week and they believed I passed the danger point and would survive. I still had mononucleosis and would need to be careful not to overdo myself. They were sending me home to recuperate and in two weeks, if all went well, I could go back to work.

I went home to my own bedroom. I looked a mess. I had half my hair. I lost my beautiful dark tan. I was left looking like a pale invalid. I was home to rest and regain my strength. During those two weeks I continued to pray and read my Bible, asking the Lord for courage to do what I needed to do. At the end of those two weeks I was ready to go back to work.

The day that I had to go back to work, I knew what was before me. I had to carry my Bible. So again, I prayed. I was determined my life belonged to Jesus, not to myself. I took my big Bible and boldly put it into my lunchbox and went to work. I kept repeating Galatians 2:20;

> *"I have been crucified with Christ and I no longer live, but Christ lives in me. The life I now live in the body, I live by faith in the Son of God, who loved me and gave himself for me."*

It was true. The old Dick LaFountain died in that hospital bed. I no longer would be allowed to live for myself but for him who died for me. As I sat in the parking lot this time I prayed and I said, "Lord I'm not going to ask you for the courage. I've already got the courage. I have to do what I have to do." So, I carried my Bible into the factory and at my lunchtime the Lord said, "I want you to open the Bible and read it." So, I opened my lunchbox, pulled up my Bible and spent my time on my breaks reading the Bible.

You need to understand that the guys at the factory were very profane. These guys cussed, swore and told dirty stories constantly. They were filthy talkers. Especially during the lunch period there were nonstop dirty stories going on. One of these guys stood out as the most wicked among them. He was very loud, vulgar and obnoxious.

When I opened my Bible to read I thought, "Lord I hope this guy doesn't see me." I could see him across the room. He kept looking at me. I prayed, "Lord don't let him come over here." But no sooner had I prayed I saw him walking across the room looking at me. I thought, "Here he comes and he's going to mock me. He's going to tell me I'm such a wimp and such a stupid Christian." Because he had done that before with other people.

But this time he came to the picnic table where I sat taking the seat on the other side of me, he looked straight into my eyes and asked, "What are you reading?" I told him I was reading my Bible. He asked, "Are you a Christian?" I responded, "Yes I am." Then he shocked me by saying, "I always wanted to know what was in the Bible but I've never read it. Could you tell me what's in the Bible? So, that night I was able to share Christ with him and tell him some of the stories of the Bible. To my surprise He did not mock me. He respected me. He thanked me for sharing that with him and I promised to give him a Bible.

Part 2

God Who Helps Me

God is our refuge and strength, a very present help in trouble. Therefore will not we fear, though the earth be removed, and though the mountains be carried into the midst of the sea; Though the waters thereof roar and be troubled, though the mountains shake with the swelling thereof. Selah.

Psalm 46:1-3

Chapter 7

God's Protection

"He will cover you with his feathers, and under his wings you will find refuge; his faithfulness will be your shield and rampart." Psalm 91:4

Hit From Behind

Psalm 5:12
*Surely, LORD, you bless the righteous; you
surround them with your favor as with a shield.*

I have a couple accident stories to tell you. Most of them have to do with Brazil, but then again we've been prone to accidents so it happens anywhere that we go. The devil is out to get you, so beware.

We were missionaries in Porto Alegre, Brazil, a large city of 1,500,000 people. We lived on the outskirts of the city on the northeastern side of town. We would often have to go downtown to do business, which was a long bus ride, or about a half hour drive by car. Once or twice a month I would make the trek downtown to pay all bills because you couldn't do it by mail. You had to do it in person at the bank, or at the electric company, or wherever you had to pay your bill. I looked forward to those times because I enjoyed going into center city. I would always treat myself to an espresso coffee, ice cream, or some special lunch when I was downtown.

One day I had spent the day downtown paying my bills, getting my hair cut, having lunch and an expresso. When I finished I left the parking garage and decided to take the roundabout way to get back home because the more direct route was through the middle of the city which got quite congested. I took the bypass going around the city. This route would save me fifteen minutes and would take me almost to our house in the northern part of the city.

This wide four-lane boulevard had traffic lights and pedestrian crosswalks. I got onto the four-lane road and was cruising along nicely, making good time. I was in the left lane of the four-lane highway when I came to a traffic light that was red, so I stopped, being the first car at the light. This was not an intersection but a pedestrian crosswalk. I remember pulling up to the stop light. I remember looking in my rearview mirror and seeing a truck some distance behind me. I also noticed there were people crossing the street in front of me. The next thing I heard was a crash and all of my windows exploded. The truck that was behind me evidently didn't have any brakes. He slammed into the back of my car going 40 or 50 miles an hour. It's quite a shock to be hit from behind like that! After he hit me I ended up in the grassy median strip with the whole back end of my car completely crushed. I sat there for a moment dazed by what had just happened. I climbed out of the car confused and disoriented. I had not seen the truck other than noticing him in my rearview mirror some distance away. I got out of the car hurting from the sudden impact. I surveyed the situation. My car was totally destroyed.

The truck was leaking radiator fluid all over the street. The driver of course was upset because his brakes didn't work. He was speaking rapidly in Portuguese and I was still upset so my Portuguese probably wasn't the best that it could have been. While I stood there an elderly man came running across the street yelling at me. He was screaming at me in Portuguese and I thought I was in serious trouble. He was asking everyone who the driver of the car was. I hesitantly admitted I was the driver. He suddenly grabbed me and began shaking my hand saying, "Thank you! Thank you! Thank you!' Then he explained that I had saved the lives of his grandchildren. They were crossing the street right in front of my car when the truck hit. He said, "Your eyes got as big as saucers and you frantically spun the steering wheel to the left avoiding hitting my grandchildren. You saved my grandchildren, that's why you ended up in the median strip. You are a hero. They would have been killed but for your quick thinking. Thank you so much." By this time he was in tears telling the police officer and the people gathered around what I had done.

After he told me this I remembered seeing the children in the street in front of my car, but when the truck hit me I just reacted. I appreciated the man complementing me and telling me what a great driver I was, but to tell the truth I was totally unaware of what took place. It's at that moment I remembered the Scripture that says, *"The angel of the Lord encamps around about them that fear him and delivers them."* I believe it was the angel of the Lord that took hold of that steering wheel and turned it in the direction it needed to go. God takes care of his children.

Marilyn and the Bus

Psalm 27:5
For in the day of trouble he will keep me safe in his dwelling; he will hide me in the shelter of his sacred tent and set me high upon a rock.

In another incident Marilyn was driving a new replacement car. Angelica was a toddler and in the car with her. I think she was on her way to pick up our children from school. She was taking a short cut on some back roads because it's easier to avoid the busy traffic on the main roads. About every block or so there was a stop sign, sometimes a four-way stop, sometimes not. This happened to be a two way stop. A tree hid the stop sign at the intersection and she failed to stop. At the same moment a bus was passing in front of her. She slammed into the side of the bus. Fortunately, there was not a great deal of damage to the bus, but our new car had a great deal of damage. Marilyn was quite upset. She got out of the car to make sure everything was okay. The bus driver told her everything was fine there was no problem with the bus and he was able to continue on his way. That left Marilyn standing in the middle of the road in an unfamiliar neighborhood confused and shaken up. She couldn't drive the car. It was undrivable. She didn't know where to turn. In those moments of confusion you really need the Lord's help. I'm sure that in her heart she was crying out to the Lord.

Just then a young man saw her and noticed her confused state. He approached to see if she was okay. He immediately recognized by her accent that she was an American, and he spoke to her in English! He asked if he could help her, maybe take her home, or whether she needed to call somebone on the telephone. He lived nearby and they had a phone. (There were no cell phones in those days.) Well, that was quite unusual because most Brazilians don't speak English, but this young man spoke American English. He took her to his house, which was just a few houses away. Marilyn found out these were American missionaries serving with the Mennonites. How gracious the Lord was to allow that accident to happen two houses from a missionary's home. We thank the Lord that nobody was injured. No one in the bus was injured. The car was damaged and I felt really bad about that. It was a brand new car. But we're so thankful the Lord protects us and cares for us in our times of need. Once again the angel of the Lord encamped around about us and delivered us.

Accident, 10 Injured

James 1:2-3
Count it all joy, my brothers, when you meet trials of various kinds, for you know that the testing of your faith produces patience.

The next accident happened in the United States. We were serving in Pitman, New Jersey pastoring a little church. Pitman is located in south Jersey where there are small private lakes. We had joined a lake swimming club and as members we were taking our children, visiting cousins, and one teenager from the church to swim. All of us were in our big Mercury Grand Marquis station wagon. As we traveled down a two-lane road going toward the lake we came to a very dangerous curve. I suddenly saw a Camaro IROC-Z sports car coming towards us at a high rate of speed. He failed to navigate the curve and lost control of his car. He side swiped the car in front of us and sent it off the road, then he careened down the middle of the roadway skidding sideways toward our car. I was traveling about 40 miles an hour. He was moving probably 60 or 70 miles an hour. As he came skidding toward us I saw there was nowhere to go. I couldn't go to the right because there was a big brick mailbox there. I couldn't go to the left because there was a deep ditch. I thought, "If he gains control he's going to go to the left of me," so I slammed on the brakes and yelled for everybody hang on. I hit his car broadside in the middle of that road. The t-top popped off and the passenger flew out of the car landing in an adjacent yard. The Camero continued sliding around us smashing into my driver side door and window.

In that panic moment all our windows broke. There was glass everywhere. The children in the backseat were screaming and crying. Marilyn was injured and in tremendous pain. She couldn't move. She couldn't even unbuckle her seatbelt. I couldn't open my door which was crushed by the Camero. He had spun around and hit the side of our car smashing the mirror and my window. Something hit and tore my ear lobe and my elbow was ripped and bleeding badly.

I eventually managed to get the door open and started pulling the children out through the broken windows. They all were bleeding badly from cuts and lacerations from the flying glass. The neighbors came from the house and began helping us pull the children out of the car.

At that point we did not know the extent of the damage and we didn't know how seriously anyone was injured. I carried the children out to the lawn where the neighbors helped them. Once they were safely on the lawn I went back to get Marilyn.

She was still sitting in the car and the car was smoking. I was afraid a spark might send the gas tank up in flames and she could be caught in the car. I kept insisting she get out of the car but she could not. She couldn't move. She said she hurt too badly. By this time somebody had called 911 and the ambulance arrived, then fire engines and emergency vehicles came. They helped Marilyn get out of the car. They put her on to a stretcher to get her into an ambulance. All of us were taken by ambulance to the nearest hospital.

We later found out the car that was run off the road had several passengers in it. One of them was a pregnant woman. She was also taken to the hospital. They were afraid she was going to go into early labor. They transported the two guys who were in the Camaro to the same hospital. I don't know if they had been drinking, but they appeared to be uninjured. Even the guy who flew out of the car and landed in the lawn seem to be uninjured.

We finally got to the emergency room and they began to treat all of our injuries. The doctors and nurses cared for the superficial wounds on the children and assured us that the children were not seriously injured. Everyone had cuts and bruises. Marilyn probably had the worst injury. She had eight cracked ribs and whiplash. We were satisfied to be able to talk back and forth between emergency bays that separated us by curtains. We knew the children were okay and were calming down. There were 10 people injured in that accident.

As we were walking out of the hospital my doctor happened to come in. He asked what had happened. He saw my ear and my head wrapped with gauze and asked what they had done for it. He looked at it and insisted I go back into the emergency room where he examined my ear and said it needed stitches. He spent time stitching up my ear and then going back to my arm and stitching it up.

The next day I went to see the car. The car was completely demolished. The front end, which had a huge eight cylinder engine, was completely compacted and crushed. The man at the body shop asked how many people died in the accident. I told him that no one had died but 10 people were injured, none seriously. He said, "That's amazing because any car that comes in like this there is usually one fatality at least. You can count your blessings that no one was seriously injured. Looking at this car you would think the front passengers would have died.

This was another one of those cases where the angel of the Lord was camping around us and delivering us. The Lord did take care of us. The children were not injured seriously. They were able to go on with life. Marilyn did not have a good summer. She had to sit up in a recliner and was not able to lay down flat because of her injuries. I had severe whiplash and had to go to a chiropractor three times a week for almost a year. Again, God took care of us in what could have been deadly.

Climbing Pike's Peak

Exodus 19:4
You have seen all that I have done to the Egyptians, and I took you up as upon eagles' wings, and I brought you near to myself.

When I moved to Colorado Springs in 1998 to work at the National Office of the Christian and Missionary Alliance hiking looked like a good idea. Colorado Springs is about 6,500 feet above sea level, making it difficult for some people to breathe easily in the thin mountain air. For me the mountain air was great. I loved hiking and my first experience above 10,000 feet was euphoric. Above the Springs stands the majestic often snow-covered Pikes Peak.

The first time Andrew and I tried climbing Pikes Peak was just before Christmas, and there was a little snow but not much. We made it about half way up, to the Barr Camp, which had taken us about 3 1/2 hours of steady climbing. We both had small backpacks. My twenty-four year old son is a jock. I am not. I had a coronary "roto-rooter" job (angioplasty with two stents put in) just a year before. I was recovered but not in the best of shape. Andrew ended up carrying my pack for the last mile and a half - OK, maybe two miles.

When I got there I was so exhausted and breathing so heavily I thought I would never be able to climb back down that day. In fact, I said as much to Andrew as I collapsed in a chair. But after resting for an hour and taking in fluids and nourishment I felt somewhat revived. When I saw the very rustic overnight accommodations I decided to try going down. We made it down much more easily. I couldn't even get out of bed the next day and I ached for days.

A few months later in May I had become more accustomed to the altitude. I had been playing racquetball several times a week, so I was in better shape than when I arrived in Colorado Springs. Andrew, always being in top form, was ready to assault the summit the moment he arrived from graduate school in England. He was determined to make it to the top this time. I did not feel in top form so I told my wife, Marilyn, when I left her off at work at 6:30 a.m. that I was sure the best I could do was to get to the A-frame cabin at the tree line.

Andrew and I started our trek at 7:30 a.m. The weather was mild, overcast with the threat of sprinkles to dampen our walk but the temperature was in the low sixties. The first couple of miles of the trail are very steep as the path zigzags up the mountain gaining altitude rather quickly. That part of the trail takes about an hour and a half of fast paced, calf-cramping, lung-bursting, heart-pounding, blood-pressure-stressing, my-head-is-dizzy, wondering-why-I-am-doing-this, kind of climb. Then we rested for 10 to 15 minutes, eating snacks and hydrating before continuing our upward climb.

The path leveled out and became a steady upward grade as we moved farther and farther from civilization. The views of the valleys and the plains below where Colorado Springs and our home lay were spectacular and so we were refreshed thinking, "This is why I love to punish myself to get up here."

For the next several miles it is uphill with woods surrounded with beautiful boulders in odd rock formations. It was beautiful scenery! Then it leveled out (that is figurative since it never is really level) into a meadow-like area with views of the peak. Finally, after hiking almost continuously for hours, except for stops to drink water, we arrived at the Barr Camp, the halfway point.

The Barr Camp is a rustic cabin where a family lives year-round to assist hikers on their way up Pikes Peak. The weather was now noticeably colder and clouds covered the peak. But there was no snow on the ground. We asked our host about the weather at the top. He radioed ahead and reported that there was sleet and snow in the forecast with wind. It was then that he cautioned us about even thinking about trying for the top. We mentioned that we wanted to keep climbing to at least get to the A-frame cabin at the tree line. His pessimistic report was that other climbers had not been able to get through. The snow was still far too deep. Reports had been coming in that it was still impassible even to the A-frame. They also said, "We don't recommend attempting the summit, at least not without the right equipment (snowshoes, etc) because there are six foot drifts up to the timberline and then snow to the top." We said, "Okay, but we'll just go a couple more miles until the snow gets too deep. We just want to see it." We signed in the guestbook and promised we would go up as far as we could and would check in on our return. We really intended to return.

So off we went. Soon we came across a guy with full equipment on his way down. He was a young guy maybe around thirty years old and built like an athlete. He had full gear: waterproof boots, trousers and jacket, cuffs around his ankles to keep the snow out, poles for balance, and snowshoes. He said, "Once you hit 10,000 feet it becomes a virtual impasse. I couldn't even get through with the snowshoes - I kept sinking into the six-foot snow and it exhausted me very quickly, so I gave up at around 11,000 ft. You can hike another mile and a half or so from here, but the summit is just not possible and it's still about 6 miles from here."

We were certain that we would never get very far, but we had already climbed to the Barr Camp once before so we wanted to at least get to the tree line (that is where vegetation stops growing, usually about 11,000 feet.) So on we trekked.

The path was pretty clear except for huge mounds of drifted snow that seemed to be only on the trail, not in the woods. The snow on the path was deep but firm from being there a long time and trampled by many footprints. We figured if there were all those footprints others must have gone this far. It couldn't be too bad. Soon we came to what appeared to be the end of the normal trail. The footprints were still in the snow, but they went in various directions. The well-equipped climber mentioned seeing those footprints too, but he was familiar with the trail and was certain they were not following the trail at that point. We later discovered he was right.

Being stout fellows and lovers of snow we plodded on traversing the deepest snow as the trail turned to the right and rose steeply uphill. When Andrew's legs went down into the snow up to his waist it became obvious that this was probably not the normal trail. We could see some fence wires along the streambed that we were following but no obvious trail. We climbed on, lumbering over soft places in the snow, often up to our knees and then sinking to our hips. From time to time we could hear a torrent of water gushing down beneath the snow. This was obviously a stream we were following, but it was a wide treeless gully so we followed on. At times it became so difficult to get past the deep soft snow that we climbed over to the rocks and jumped from rock to rock. We grabbed low hanging tree branch to tree branch until it was passable again. Then we returned to the soft snow of the streambed.

It was beautiful and we love snow. If we had a sled we would have had a really great time. In due course we came to an opening and could see the treeline above us. That spurred us on! At the treeline the view opened up so we could see the top of Pike's Peak. We could see laterally to the north and south of us too. Then looking back toward the plains we had a fabulous view of Colorado Springs far below us now. Wow! This view itself was worth the climb.

We looked around for the A-frame cabin but it was nowhere to be found. But there stood Pike's Peak right in front of us. We could still see footprints leading straight on up the gully to the top. We occasionally stopped on some large boulders for a snack of dried bananas, raisins and M&Ms. There the birds flew right up and grabbed nuts and raisins right out of our hands. This was a paradise!

As we surveyed our locale we decided to go up a little higher where we might be able to look back and see the A-frame we had missed. The higher we got the more beautiful it became. It was so quiet. You could understand why mountain men have chosen to live alone in the wonder of these rocks and woods.

By this time it was approaching 12:30 and we had to make a decision to go on or turn back. I was in favor of turning back, having not found the A-frame, and conscious of my tired legs and the long walk back down the trail. Andrew however, being young and energetic, and having come all the way from England with so very few chances to be this close to the summit, urged for going on to the top. "Look, Dad" he said, "It's right in front of us. It can't be that far!" I cautioned Andrew that distances could be deceiving at these altitudes, but not wanting to ruin his hike, and not wanting him to go on alone (which he would have done I am sure) I hesitantly agreed to press on for the summit. After all, we had all afternoon in front of us and certainly the worst was behind us. It did look rather close from where we were standing. (In fact it was about four miles of steep 45 to 60 degree grade to climb.) I suppose it appeared so close because there were no trees or objects by which to judge distance. Also, there were those pockmarks in the snow. We were sure they were footprints and we could see they went straight up the mountain toward the summit. So, "Dumb and Dumber" continued on.

Soon those footprints were no longer clear footprints. Maybe they never were. The altitude does strange things to your mind. Now they appeared to be just pockmarks in the snow, but we thought they were footprints. The more we climbed the less clear the footprints became. Our breathing was definitely more labored now. We were well above the treeline and ascending steeply. From time to time we would stop for a drink, rest and eat something. Not that we had any appetite. Mostly we just knew that we needed the food for energy to keep going.

Andrew led the way. He often would follow pockmarks that took him far to the left or right of the center line only to find the side trails were no easier. We had to jam our feet into the snow to get a foothold. I was thankful for Andrew's footprints ahead of me. It made my climb easier, except that his stride was bigger than mine. I couldn't always put my feet into his footprints. The slope was difficult enough to climb, but adding to our misery was the fact that the snow was crusted with ice making it difficult to take a firm step forward. We had to stomp with each step to get a foothold in the snow and keep from sliding backward.

In the thin air above 12,000 feet this kind of action saps your strength in a hurry. I found that at times I could only take one or two steps then stop, lean over, catch my breath then take a few more steps. The weather was getting worse. Instead of raindrops, snow flurries pelted us as we climbed. The wind began blowing gusty and strong. Now it was no longer wet snow but ice hard compact snow. The temperature was well below freezing now. It was getting very cold. I remembered hearing that the temperature on the mountain would drop below zero at night.

Our shoes and jeans were wet from climbing through so much wet snow. Neither of us had boots. Mine were a pair of hiking sneakers (not waterproof), and Andrew's were similar but high tops. We had worn just jeans, t-shirts, a long-sleeved shirt, and a jacket. I carried a hooded sweatshirt since I don't like the cold winds on the mountains blowing down my neck. Andrew had worn just a light windbreaker jacket over his shirt. I had left my down-filled jacket in the car thinking it was too warm for it, and we were certainly not going to the top.

Andrew was much colder than me. I was sweating profusely from the exertion of climbing. Andrew was getting quite cold. My first hint of trouble was when he complained about his feet being wet and cold. I had not even noticed my cold feet until he mentioned it. When we stopped to sit on a rock we noticed the wind had picked up and clouds were now building over us. Andrew was visibly shivering. In spite of the cold we were sweating from the exertion of climbing this monster mountain. I had put extra socks, double pairs, in my pack. So we sat on the rock and changed our socks. That helped immediately. Then we realized that if we put our shoes back on the socks would soon be as wet as the others. Digging into my trusty backpack we found some plastic grocery bags and put them around our dry socks before inserting our feet in our soaked shoes. That helped Andrew with his cold feet. I had taken thick ski gloves with me. Andrew had not.

We climbed on until 3 o'clock. We were beyond exhausted and we were getting concerned. We expected to catch the cog rail train down from the summit but we were not sure when the last one left. I was thinking it was 5:30 p.m. but was not sure, was it 4:30 or 5:30?

The more we climbed the farther the Peak seemed to be. It was getting closer but the climb was getting harder and noticeably steeper! We had not planned on this. We also thought that we would have crossed the regular trail and would be able to follow that more easily to the top, but no trail.

By 3:30 we were so exhausted and out of breath that we were getting sick. I got cramps and diarrhea along the trail. (Fortunately again I brought a roll of toilet paper and plastic bags to carry it out in.) Andrew had a splitting headache and nausea. Neither of us wanted to eat anything. Now we were worried! The steepest part of the climb was still ahead of us and it really did look impassable! There was deep snow and getting deeper with huge rocks ahead to climb over. I was at the point of panic.

I knew I could not make the rest of this climb without supernatural intervention. I began to cry out to God -- "O God, what have we done! Please send a helicopter, or someone to save us. We are in big trouble. We need help. We may not get out of this alive. If we miss that train we may have to spend the night on top, and the temperature still drops below zero! O Lord, have mercy. O Lord hear and answer, please." Then I began to pray with each step. "O Lord, give us the wings of eagles."

By this time we could only go a few feet and stop to bend over to catch our breath. I hated this snow! Every step was a labor. These sneakers were not made for high mountain snow trekking.

Finally we could see the train in the distance. Certainly they could see us! But they couldn't. We were like tiny ants on the mountain side. I began to call out loud "Hello! Can anybody hear us! We need help!" Of course no one could hear us. They were on top and we were over a steep embankment from where they were. The snow now was so deep we gave up on it and went toward the steep rocks instead. Perhaps they would be easier to scale -- NOT! The rocks were steep, wet, and slippery. There was no other way to the top and it was too late in the day to start back down. So we pressed on.

By this time I was in front and Andrew was following. I was worried about him. He kept complaining about his headache, and that is not like Andrew. I knew he was suffering from altitude sickness but what else could we do but press on. I was also aware that if either of us fell there would be no stopping our fall, gravity and the wind would take us down the mountain.

About this time we caught a glimpse of the corner of the observation tower and a woman was standing there looking out over the mountains. I shouted more "hellos" but no one saw or heard us.

The path had gone almost vertical on us. Andrew was sure an angel kept him from falling backward and down onto rocks. At one point his head went fuzzy and light and his body leaned back and he would have fallen backward, but at that moment he felt as though a hand was placed on his back and instead of falling back he leaned forward. Later, when we reached the top he thanked me for pushing him against the rock when he was falling. I said, "Andrew, I was in front of you. I never pushed you against the rock."

We climbed over another section of boulders and we could see the roof of the summit house. The last few hundred yards we climbed almost straight up on our hands and knees. We climbed over the last steep boulders to the top and there directly in front of us was the train! What a welcome sight!

We staggered into the summit store to get warm and get tickets before the train left. While we were negotiating for one-way tickets down the announcement was made that the last train was leaving at 4:40. (It was 4:30 when we stepped over the tracks) All those who came in cars would have to leave as the store was closing too. Andrew and I felt like crying. We had made it! Both of us had kept quiet about our desperate fears and silently called on the Lord to save us. He did. We will be forever grateful. There is no bragging about making it to the top.

When we boarded the train the conductor came around and saw our backpacks and drenched clothes. He asked where we had been. We told him we climbed Pike's Peak. He said that was impossible. No one could get through the trail. We said, we know. We didn't use the trail. We came straight up the mountain. He suggested we call the newspaper to tell this story. We said, "No! Please, don't tell anyone what we've done."

It was a dumb thing to do when warned by experienced climbers not to try. God was gracious to us, to our families, and to the rescue rangers who would have had to pick up our frozen carcasses in the morning. So ends the adventure of a lifetime.

Twice since then I have been back to the top of Pikes Peak, once by car, once climbing the real trail. Each time I was again astounded at the impossibly steep snow-covered rocks we climbed over to get to the top just in the nick of time. Once I descended the peak, hiking down. Along the way I stopped to tell hikers our story and show them the path we took. As we stood like dwarfs among those boulders I again reveled at the miracle of God's care. Each time they would give me a curious look and slowly smile saying, "You're making that up aren't you?" I would affirm it to be true, but inevitably they would look back at the trail we took and shaking their heads saying, "Impossible, absolutely impossible, nobody could do that." As I meandered my way down the mountain, with tears in my eyes, again and again, I too looked back, shook my head and said, "Yes Lord, it is impossible. But you gave us the wings of eagles!"

Chapter 8

God's Providences

"He will cover you with his feathers, and under his wings you will find refuge; his faithfulness will be your shield and rampart."
Psalm 91:4

The righteous person may have many troubles, but the LORD delivers him from them all. Psalm 34:19

God Healed My Truck

1 Thessalonians 5:18
*In everything give thanks; for this is the
will of God in Christ Jesus for you.*

Here's a story that I've told many times as I preach sermons and share what God has done in our lives. I have had men come up to me after telling this story and accuse me of being a liar, that God doesn't and can't heal cars. My answer to that is that he has healed mine on many occasions, but I'm sorry that He hasn't done it for you.

I was in Uniontown, Pennsylvania for a weekend conference. I spoke at the men's group on a Saturday morning. I was on my way back to my motel. I expected to have a free afternoon where I could focus on preparing my mind and heart for the next full day of preaching and teaching on prayer. Uniontown is in a hilly area with some very steep inclines. As I approached my motel on the top of a hill there was a traffic light. When the light changed I was to turn left to go into the parking lot of the motel. Suddenly my truck decided to stall right in the intersection. Of course, to make matters worse my truck was standard shift. I had to put my foot on the clutch pedal and the brake at the same time to keep from rolling backwards and try to start the truck. It wouldn't start.

My 1998 Chevy S-10 was a wonderful truck and had given me many years of service without any trouble whatsoever. So, I was a little confused when my truck suddenly wouldn't start. I spent a few moments there at the traffic light with horns honking as I tried to get the car started. It would turn over and just sputter but not quite start. I was finally able to get it started but it was running very rough. I got through the traffic light and into the parking lot.

Needless to say, I was very frustrated that my truck chose this inopportune moment to start acting up. I've often observed that when you're doing the work of God Satan will put all kinds of obstacles in your way. This is particularly true when you are preaching on prayer or on overcoming the devil. Things that normally would be quite easy become very difficult and things that don't normally go wrong will suddenly go very wrong.

I wasn't too concerned about the truck so I went into the motel and put my belongings down, had my lunch and took a nap. I thought I'd just rest and the truck would cool down and be fine in just a few hours. I thought maybe it just overheated from navigating the steep hills in Uniontown.

About 2 o'clock in the afternoon I got up from my nap and went out to the car and breathed a little prayer for the truck to start. I tried the truck again with the same results. It turned over "rev, rev, rev, rev, rev, rev" but it wouldn't catch. It would cough and start to catch, but then it would quit.

I didn't know exactly what to do so I went back into the motel and called the pastor. I asked if he might have a mechanic or somebody that works in a gas station that might take a look at my car. He said unfortunately it was a holiday weekend and all the mechanics were away. I was left to try to figure out the problem by myself. I am not a mechanic. I certainly don't know anything about engines and how to get them started. So, I did what I normally do, I prayed. I asked the Lord if He would cause the truck to start to function normally to save me a frustrating afternoon. Well, that was not the way it was going to work.

To get the proper picture here you have to understand that I was at least two hours from my home in Grove City. If I had to leave my truck with a mechanic on Monday my wife would have to come pick me up then drive back to Grove City. Then when the truck was repaired we would have to drive back to Uniontown on Tuesday or Wednesday. That would be a lot of driving and the expense of getting the truck fixed.

In my mind I was anticipating all of these confusing events and the expense, which I couldn't afford, and realized life was going to be very difficult for a couple of days. I called my wife and told her what was going on. I asked her to pray and ask the Lord to allow the truck to somehow get started so I could get home.

During the afternoon I periodically went out to the truck and tried to start it. Of course I would pray beforehand asking the Lord to make it start. But it wouldn't. I saw a gas station across the street that had no garage but a convenience store. I went over and I looked at some of the car care products they had on their shelves. They had some gas additives that you put into your gas tank that was supposed to help your car run smoothly, so I thought may that would help.

I went back to the truck, put the gas treatment into the tank, waited a while, and I tried starting it. It still would not start. I thought I'll just let it rest awhile. Perhaps the additive needed time to cycle through the engine I waited about an hour then went back to try it again. The truck still would not start, in fact the battery was dying and matters were getting worse.

Then I really started to worry and fret. How was I going to get back home and get this thing fixed without a lot of expense and trouble? I called my wife again and asked her to really pray that God would do something so I wouldn't be stuck here. It could cost us hundreds of dollars to get this thing fixed and if we had to have it towed all the way back to Grove City that was really going to be very expensive.

I went back inside to try to meditate and think about my sermons and teaching lectures. While I was doing that the Lord reminded me of some of the things I was teaching.

I had been teaching about prayer and I was teaching about praise. I was teaching about being thankful in all circumstances and about worship. The Lord reminded me that I hadn't been thankful at all. I had been worrying and complaining about the truck and its inability to start. I had forgotten all the good times I had with this truck. I had forgotten that for at least eight years this truck had run beautifully without any problems. The Lord spoke to me that afternoon and said, "Why don't you try thanksgiving? Why don't you be thankful as you have been teaching others? *"In everything give thanks for this is the will of God in Christ Jesus concerning you."*

Don't you hate it when God wants you to do something very practical when you're frustrated? I was being very grumpy and dissatisfied. It was really upsetting my Saturday afternoon which in turn would upset me for Sunday morning by not having my mind prepared for the messages that would follow the next day. After thinking about it for a while and being under conviction that it was true, I agreed. I was not thankful, not in the least.

After settling that I need to be thankful I told the Lord I was sorry and I would try to be thankful in everything. I went out to the truck again and I walked around it. I actually put my hands on it, walked around it, and talked out loud and said, "Truck I really love you. You've been a great truck. You've served me well." Then I reviewed in my mind some of the things that have happened with the truck and how God has enabled me to use it without any trouble. As I did that I was really starting to feel the praise and thanksgiving welling up in my heart. I found myself thankful for the good times that God had given me.

I probably spent 20 minutes to a half hour walking around the truck and being thankful. After that I sat in the truck for a while and just praised the Lord giving thanks for His goodness and faithfulness. Then as I leaned over the steering wheel I whispered a prayer. "Dear Lord I really am thankful and I thank you for this truck and I thank you for the blessings you've given me through it and I thank you that you're able to do immeasurably more than we ask or think and even though the truck doesn't start I am determined that I'm going to give you thanks anyway for you do all things well...but it would certainly be a wonderful gift of

God that you allow this truck to start and allow me to get home without any trouble."

At that point I put the key in the ignition and low and behold the engine started. It was no longer running rough. It was not sputtering and it was not stalling. There was nothing wrong with the engine. It was as if nothing bad had ever happened.

I decided I would go out and drive around a little. I did some shopping, got my supper and came back to the motel. Still nothing was wrong with that truck whatsoever. God healed my truck!

Is God able to heal mechanical troubles? Does God heal Chevy S-10's? My answer to that is, yes he does. No, he doesn't always do it. And no, He doesn't always bail us out when we need a miracle. But there are times that God is working something in our hearts that needs to be done and He is willing and able to do immeasurably more than we ask or even imagine.

God Heals a Car
Psalm 34:19
*Many are the afflictions of the righteous,
but the Lord delivers him out of them all.*

I might add to the story that that was not the only time God has healed a car or a mechanical vehicle. While I was in college five of my friends and I were traveling back from Nyack, New York to Toledo, Ohio in my friend's Corvair. This was before route 80 was completed. There were lots of back road detours to get around the portions that were not completed.

It was probably about one or two o'clock in the morning when we were on one of those back hilly road detours that the Corvair for some unknown reason stopped and would not start. My friend was able to pull over to the side of the road on a very dark and dangerous spot in the roadway. He tried the car but it kept stalling. It wouldn't start. It wouldn't turn over. It wouldn't do anything. It was dead. We didn't know what to do. We opened the hood. The guys all messed around wiggling wires. We would have tried jumper cables, but there was no one around to jump the car. This was before the day of cell phones, so we couldn't call for help. We were getting very frustrated.

One of my friends was a little more mechanical than the rest of us and was able to look at the air filter and a few other things. We had a flashlight so he even checked the points to see if they were right.

Everything seemed to be fine, but there was nothing that we could do. We sat there for an hour. As we sat there that hour wondering what to do one of my friends said, "Why don't we pray?" I don't know why prayer seems to be the last thing that comes to our minds when we have these kinds of mechanical problems. Perhaps it's that we believe God helps those who help themselves. Or maybe we don't believe God can heal mechanical issues.

God showed us as we sat in the car that we were to pray and praise the Lord. Each of us prayed a little prayer asking the Lord to somehow heal this car and make it run properly. We finished our prayer time and my friend put the key in the ignition and turned it over and the Corvair started! It ran just fine. We drove all the way to Toledo, Ohio that night and he had no more trouble with it, He dropped my friend off in Toledo then he dropped me off in Monroe, Michigan and then he went on to Dearborn where he lived. He had no more car trouble. I saw him when we got back to college and he said, "You know I had no more mechanical problems with that car. God healed my Corvair!"

Engine Freezes Up

1 Peter 4:12
Beloved, do not be surprised at the fiery trial when it comes upon you to test you, as though something strange were happening to you.

There was another incident that took place that I'm embarrassed to tell you about because it was entirely my fault. I was delinquent in taking care of my car properly. You have to understand, we were earning a mere $75 a week, so I didn't have any money to spare for scheduling proper maintenance. It was my Galaxy 500. We had just finished our Thanksgiving eve service and somebody had given us a $25 gift. We decided that was enough to get us to Michigan to visit my family and then turn around and come back for Sunday services that weekend.

We drove to Michigan and had a wonderful time with family. After Thanksgiving was over we decided to drive back late on a Saturday in order to get back for church on Sunday. While we were traveling on the Ohio Turnpike the car engine began to knock very heavily. It sounded like there was something seriously wrong with it. We pulled off at one of the rest areas that had a gas station hoping someone on duty could help us figure out what was wrong. Well, nobody had any solutions and nobody had any mechanic on duty on a holiday weekend. We had to get off the turnpike and look for a gas station with a garage to help. We inquired at several places if there was a mechanic on duty that could help us find the problem. No mechanics were available on a holiday weekend.

So, we had no choice but to drive on hoping to get home safely. Soon the check oil light went on and began blinking at us. I checked the oil level to see if it needed more, but it seemed to be full. I even bought some more oil and poured some STP into the engine as well. We drove from the middle of Ohio all the way back to Clymer, Pennsylvania, all the while praying that the Lord would somehow get us home safely or provide a mechanic that could fix our car since no garages were open that weekend.

We got to Pennsylvania driving the back roads to get to Clymer. By then the car was really making a racket. It felt like it was falling apart, like the whole thing was going to blow up on us. We prayed and asked the Lord to help us get home. We entered our back driveway and pulled up to the garage and stopped. Immediately the engine quit and wouldn't start again. It had completely frozen up.

God allowed us to get home safely and we were glad. We were able to get back for Sunday morning services. We knew that we had an expensive repair to do on the car and had to have it towed somewhere. As I said, we were not wealthy, we made $75 a week and that was not much even back then in the early 70's. We had no extra cash, that's why $25 as a gift was given to us so we could go to Michigan. We were able to arrange a tow to get the car to the next town with a Ford dealer to look it over.

When we finally got the call from the Ford Dealer he was very upset. He said, "Young man do you realize what happened here? You have not changed oil and filter in your car for a long time. The oil was so dirty it clogged up the oil pump so that oil could not circulate. While you were traveling the oil pump couldn't pump the oil so your engine was running without oil for at least 300 miles. It was a miracle that you ever got home safely."

I tell you that story not because I'm proud of it but because God is merciful and gracious to those who are stupid, those who are less than careful, and those who are not mechanical. Even in our stupidity God is gracious and good. When we make mistakes, and even when it's our fault, God is faithful to protect us.

"When God put a calling on your life He already factored in you stupidity."
-- Graham Cooke

Our Crazy Opel

James 1:12
*Blessed is the man who remains steadfast under trial,
for when he has stood the test he will receive the crown of life,
which God has promised to those who love him.*

While we were students at Nyack College Marilyn and I got married in our junior year. The next year we had a child so we were living off campus in a ranch type home in a basement apartment of one of our college professors. My parking place was across the street in a gravel spot next to the road. It was not in a convenient place to park or to work on a car.

I had purchased a 1968 Opel. It was an attractive little car. It gave me good gas mileage. It did everything I wanted it to do except for a couple things.

First, if it rained, or it was foggy or humid, it would not start. I took it to the Buick dealer to have it looked at. They said unfortunately this was a trait of this 1968 Opel. They tried a tune up, changing the spark plugs and wires, resetting the points and changing the distributor cap. Nothing helped. They suggested that we spray some silicone on the distributor cap and if all else failed not to drive it when it rained.

Second, the Opel was a stick shift and the clutch was going bad. Again, not being a mechanic I took it down to the Buick dealer to have them look at it. They told me the clutch was burned out and needed to be replaced at the cost of $600. That was way more than this college student could afford, so I had to look for another less expensive solution.

I was working a full-time school custodian job at night. We had college friends that were working with us who knew mechanical things. One friend suggested that I could change the clutch myself. Another had been a mechanic and he said he would give me step by step instructions and guide me through the process. I decided I could probably do that if I parked the car far enough off the road not to interfere with the traffic that the zoomed by. I could probably buy the clutch and do it myself. So, that's what I did. I went down to the Buick dealer and found the price of the clutch was going to be $42 .

I would have to work on this car out in the open air without a garage and without a lot of mechanical tools. I also needed to find a time to do it while the weather was mild. It was the fall of the year and I decided this was a good time to begin the process.

I followed the list my mechanical friend gave me and was successful and quite pleased with myself for getting the clutch out. It took me several hours over a two or three day period, but I was successful. Next, I needed to go to town to buy the clutch and clutch plate. Having no other transportation I walked a mile down the long hill to the Buick dealer in Nyack to buy the materials.

I happened to be wearing coveralls that someone loaned me. These were long overalls mechanics use with lots of pockets for tools. Marilyn gave me the money from our little budgeting envelopes. It was exactly $42, two twenties and two ones. I tucked it into my coverall pocket and made my long trek to town.

I got to the Buick dealer, walked in, told him what I needed, gave him the parts number, and he brought the clutch out to me. I reached in my pocket to pay for it and discovered the money was not there. I didn't realize coveralls had holes for you to hang your tools as well as real pockets. I had put the money into the bottomless pocket!

I lost the only $42 we had for this project. Our budget envelopes were empty after paying all our bills. I walked a mile up the hill to get back to the college and our home praying all the way. I looked diligently in every gutter and bush to find where the money might have fallen out. I called Marilyn's brother who was also at the college to help me out. We prayed about it and decided to walk together looking on both sides of the road. He was looking on one side; I was looking on the other. The wind was blowing about twenty miles an hour so we had little hope of finding it unless the Lord would provide.

Bill eventually yelled, "I found a $20 bill!" Praise the Lord! There was hope after all. A little while later I found another $20 bill in the bushes in the opposite direction the wind was blowing. We never did find the two dollar bills, but my brother-in-law loaned me two dollars so I could get the clutch and finish. We were overjoyed with the miracle that God provided in finding that money.

I made my way back up the hill and tried to finish the job replacing the clutch. The story is not over. The weather suddenly turned cold and snowy and I was outside in the street trying to fix my car. In freezing weather, exposed to the wind and snow, I got the clutch plate attached. Next came the clutch itself. It had to be placed in between the flywheel and clutch plate before tightening it down. That's when I realized I didn't have the tool I needed to align the clutch to the clutch plate. It had to be exactly in the center and required a special tool.

I talked to my friend and he told me there was a tool that I would need to borrow from the Buick dealer. Again I walked down to the Buick dealer and asked if I could borrow the tool to align the clutch and clutch plate. They refused to loan me the tool, but they would sell it to me for $100. Well, I couldn't buy it so I walked back up the hill. I went to work the next day and told my friend what the problem was. He said there was another way. You could actually design your own tool whittling it of wood. It wouldn't be perfect but it would line it up to the center. I got it pretty well lined up.

There were six bolts to hold the clutch plate to the flywheel. In my hurry I over tightened one of the bolts and it sheered off. The next night I told my friend what happened. He asked how many bolts were on there and I said well I think there were six. He explained that I would have to buy a tap set to get the old bolt out and then re-tap it and put in an oversized screw. Then he said, "I'll tell you what. It won't be a problem if you just leave it with five bolts. That would be more than enough to hold the clutch plate on." So that's what I did. I put it all back together in a snowstorm and finally got the Opel back together. It ran fine for a few more years until I traded it for another car.

Four Flats in One Day

1 Peter 1:6-7
In all this you greatly rejoice, though now for a little while you may have had to suffer grief in all kinds of trials. These have come so that the proven genuineness of your faith—of greater worth than gold, which perishes even though refined by fire—may result in praise, glory and honor when Jesus Christ is revealed.

When you're doing God's work there are lots of things that go wrong. When you're working in Brazil, which is a spiritist culture, you can be sure that the devil is involved in making many things go wrong.

It wasn't uncommon in Brazil for us to get flat tires. There were many horse drawn carts on the roads that the poorer classes used to transport building supplies. The horses often threw a shoe and the nails ended up in the road and people got flat tires. So for us it was not unusual to have a flat tire. We would change it and go to the tire shop to have it repaired.

One particular day stands out in my memory because it involved at least four flat tires in the same day. It happened to be a time when college youth corp workers came from the United States to help us with our ministry. The first flat took place as I went to cross the town, which was around 15 miles to pick up our children from school. On the way I had a flat tire. I had to change the tire for the spare and drop the original off to be repaired. All this made me late for picking the kids up from school.

I took the kids back home and stopped at a tire shop to pick up the repaired tire. Then Marilyn needed the car to go across town to a ladies meeting. On her way to the meeting she had a flat tire. She was able to find a phone and called me to let me know what was happening. I said there wasn't much I could do about it, not having another car. She eventually found somebody to help change the tire. When she got back I took it to the tire store to be repaired. That was flat tire number two.

Then the evening came when the youth corps workers were coming in by the bus and needed to be picked up at the bus station. On the way to the bus station I had another flat tire, making me late picking them up. We got to the bus station and were able to pick up the four youth workers putting their luggage high on the roof rack of the car. Imagine five big people with their luggage packed in and on top of a small car. I mentioned to them that we already had three flats that day. As we sat in the parking lot packing things into the car I could hear a hissing sound of air leaking out of the tire, and I had no spare to change it.

I told them what we had been through that day with three flat tires already and the fourth one was deflating. It was already late at night. We were about 25 miles from center city and had to go through the entire city to get to the other side of the town where our home was. I said, "Guys we need a miracle. We have to make it home on this tire. It's the middle of the night. It's dangerous on the streets of Porto Alegre and there's no place to get a tire repaired at this time of night."

We drove all the way praying that God would enable that tire to stay inflated until we got to our house. Thankfully we made it to our house. As we pulled into the driveway I got out of the car and I stood there with the four students and said, "Listen!" We all listened as the last air escaped from that tire and it went flat.

It seems like a small thing that one would have four flat tires in one day. But it illustrates the difficulties of working as a missionary in a culture of spiritism and the occult. Satan opposes the work of ministry. He can do it through electronics, he can do it through flat tires, through people, or through life events. He is going to hinder you in any way he can.

Chapter 9

God's Provisions

"My God shall supply all your needs according to his riches in glory by Christ Jesus." – Philippians 4:19

Miraculous Bread

Psalm 37:5
I was young and now I am old, yet I have never seen the righteous forsaken or their children begging bread.

The most remarkable miracle of my life was the day God provided bread from an empty cupboard. My dad must have been on strike or laid off again because food was in short supply around our house. In the same time period Mom would give us dry milk and pretend that it was the real stuff. We always knew the difference and to this day I hate 1% or 2% milk. It reminds me of that dry milk. I remember Mom not having milk one morning so we had to have our oatmeal with water! Yuk!!! On another ominous day we didn't have any bread in the house. There was nothing to eat. Mom sat us down at breakfast and told us we were out of food.

She told us the story of George Mueller and how he prayed for food for his orphanage and God always provided. One day they had no food to feed the orphanage children. Here is his story.

> *Early one morning Mueller arrived in the dining hall for breakfast. The plates and cups or bowls were on the table. There was nothing on the table but empty dishes. There was no food in the larder, and no money to supply the need. The children were standing waiting for breakfast. 'Children, you know we must be in time for school,' said Mueller. Then lifting his hand he prayed, 'Dear Father, we thank Thee for what Thou art going to give us to eat.' According to the account, a knock was then heard at the door. The baker stood there. 'Mr Mueller, I couldn't sleep last night. Somehow I felt you didn't have bread for breakfast, and the Lord wanted me to send you some. So I got up at two o'clock and baked some fresh bread, and have brought it.' Mueller thanked the baker and praised God for His care. 'Children,' he said, 'we not only have bread, but the rare treat of fresh bread.' Almost immediately there came a second knock at the door. This time it was the milkman who announced that his milk cart had broken down outside the orphanage, and that he would like to give the children his cans of fresh milk, so that he could empty his wagon and repair it.*

My mom believed God loved us and would provide for us too. That morning as we sat at the kitchen table she prayed. She asked the Lord for a miracle for her children just as He had for George Mueller's children. Then we waited. Mom fully expected a knock at the door with a supply of food for the day. No one came. She prayed again and we waited. Nothing happened, no one called and no supplies came to our house. We had already watched Mom look through all the cupboards. We all searched the kitchen with her for something to eat. There was nothing. Old Mother Hubbard went to the cupboard, but this time it wasn't the dog without a bone, it was the kids who were going to go hungry.

Again we prayed and waited. Three times we prayed and waited, then searched again. Finally Mom got up one more time and searched again for something to feed her children. This time to all of our amazement there was a loaf of bread tucked in a corner that had not been there before. We had all searched the cupboards. We knew there was no food there. Then there was – just one loaf of bread. That morning we had toast for breakfast. We had no margarine or butter so we used Crisco lard on our bread. But we were thankful.

I wish I could go back for a video replay of that scene. We were all astounded. Someone had heard me tell this story and asked if it was a package of "Wonder Bread." It certainly was manna from heaven.

A Brand New Computer

Psalm 37:5
Commit thy way unto the LORD*; trust also in him;*
and he shall bring it to pass.

One of my favorite experiences of God's provision is a story that took place in Washington, Pennsylvania. I had been working on researching unreached people groups and writing profiles of those groups. Simply stated, an **unreached or least-reached people** *is a people group among which there is no indigenous community of believing Christians with adequate numbers and resources to evangelize this people group without outside assistance.*

I had been doing this since 1985 while in Pitman and continued in Washington. It was then 1995. I was using an old 80's computer. It was difficult to use and had unusual sized discs for saving information. It was slow and outdated. It wasn't compatible with other computers and I could not do graphics with it. I couldn't do Internet searches so I was in need of an upgraded IBM compatible computer.

I had written and compiled over 2000 profiles of unreached people groups. I had been praying about it and telling the Lord that I had been doing this now for 10 years and I needed a better computer. I desperately needed an upgraded computer so I could complete this task. I told the Lord that if this was what He wanted me to be doing then He needed to provide a better computer. I had done my shopping for computers through the then popular *Computer Shopper magazine* and had found a computer that really would service me well. It cost about $1,000. I didn't have $1,000 to buy it, so I cut out a picture of the computer and put it on my prayer bulletin board. It was a very specific request for that computer.

A few months after I started praying for this, I was visiting an elderly shut-in lady from our church. When I finished praying with her and serving communion she handed me an envelope with a check for the church and said, "This is my offering and my tithe for the church." Then she had another envelope and said, "Pastor this is for you. It's not for the church. It's for you personally. God told me to give it to you." I thanked her and said goodbye. When I got home Marilyn wasn't there but I thought I should open up the envelope and see what it was. I opened up the envelope and amazingly there was a check for $1000.

I was like a guy that won the lottery. I walked around the house shouting "Hallelujah and praise the Lord. God answered prayer!" Marilyn came home and I shared with her what God had given us and she said, "Praise the Lord I've been praying for $1,000 for some urgent home needs we have."

I was frustrated. I had prayed for this $1,000. This was my priority. I was doing God's work. This was not some frivolous household thing for the family. As we talked about it, thought about it, and debated it, the Lord finally told me to let it go.

Let it go. Let it go? How can I just let go of a thousand dollars that I prayed for? I went to my study and prayed. I wept. I cried out to the Lord, "This is what I've been praying for. How can it be that somebody else is going to take it away?" As I prayed I sensed the Lord say again, "Let it go." In the end I resolved to let it go to the family need. I wrote in my journal that I received $1,000 in answer to prayer, and then I had to give it up, so God must have something better. I continued to pray. Another six months passed.

About that time I got a phone call from a young man from our church. He was in the hospital and said he wanted me to come and visit him. He wanted to tell me what happened to him that night in the hospital. I found this 26 year old business man sitting up in bed with a nice laptop. I sat down and he told me his story.

He told me that he had gotten very sick a couple of days before. They rushed him to the hospital. The doctors did all kinds of tests to find out what was wrong. The doctor had said he didn't know what he had but it looked very serious and was life threatening. The young man was facing a critical issue of life and death. That night, he said, as he was praying Jesus came into the room and talked to him about his sin. He asked the Lord to forgive him for his many sins and for not walking more closely to the Lord. Then the Lord Jesus reached out, touched him and healed him.

Then he paused and continued, "Pastor, this is why I called you. Before Jesus left my room He turned back to me and said, 'Pastor LaFountain has a need and I want you to provide it for him.'"

He looked at me and stated, "Pastor, Jesus told me you have a need. He also said it did not have anything to do with your church work. It is something to do with a ministry the Lord has given you. I need to ask you, what is that need?"

He knew nothing about my unreached people groups, but he said the Lord told him to provide whatever it is I had been praying for. I laughed and said "Well, I've been praying for a Lamborghini. We laughed together. "No, I'm serious," he said. "The Lord says I am to provide you what you need and have been praying for. I'm going to provide it whatever it costs." Reluctantly, I told him the story of my research on unreached people groups and my need for a better computer and software. As I finished that story he showed me his expensive business laptop and asked it if would do. But I answered, "No, what I need is a desktop computer so I can do color graphics, scan pictures and download images so I can get the images of unreached people groups into the files."

He asked me to leave the room while he talked to his wife. I left the room and I waited outside for five minutes until they called me back in. Smiling he said, "Pastor my wife and I have talked about this and we know that God has ordained for us to provide for you, so here's what I'm going to ask you to do. I want you to go out and find the very best computer that you can buy, the monitor, the computer, the scanner, the printer, the software, and everything that you need in that computer. Spare no expense. Money is not an issue. I will pay for it whatever it costs."

I was blown away. I went home and pored over my *Computer Shopper* magazine for another couple weeks until I found all the items I needed and ordered them. I handed the bill to him and he paid for it. I still have the receipt today. It came to $5,500. God provided every dime.

A Prayer Cottage

2 Corinthians 9:8
God is able to bless you abundantly, so that in all things at all times, having all that you need, you will abound in every good work.

While we ministered in Grove City, Pennsylvania God gave me a burden for prayer. I was preparing to write a book titled, *Spending Time Alone With God*. We were teaching about prayer and practical prayer disciplines to our church. We conducted church prayer retreats where we would spend Friday evening and all of Saturday at a church camp learning about and practicing prayer. Twice a year we had anywhere from 25 to 45 people involved.

I had also been teaching my pastoral staff to spend time alone with God and led them on staff retreats for prayer and vision quests. They were to get away alone with God three times each year. I encouraged them to find a quiet retreat center where they could spend two or three days in prayer.

As we were doing these retreats Marilyn and I thought about what we'd like to do in retirement. We both wanted to have a retreat available for people that wanted to get away for 24 or 48 hours just to be alone with God.

On one of our pastoral prayer retreats we were walking around the campground as we prayed. One of my assistant pastors met an elderly woman who asked him if he knew anybody that wanted a cottage. Of course he was interested. He also wanted a prayer cottage. He said he was interested, but wanted to know what it would cost and what it looked like. She said she just wanted to give it away. She was too old to take care of the cottage and wanted someone who would use it. Then she showed it to him.

It was in bad shape, the roof caved in, there was black mold everywhere, the chipmunks, mice and other critters had invaded the cottage. It needed a huge amount of work. This woman gave her cottage to Bill and he began the process of cleaning it up.

Unfortunately, two years later Bill ended up with terminal cancer before he could finish the cottage. He called me to his bedside one day and handed me the keys to the cottage and he said, "Pastor, we both have been praying for a prayer cottage. I'm going home to be with the Lord. I am giving you the keys. I'm asking you to take the cottage and make it into prayer retreat cottage."

That is how God provided a prayer cottage for us. After I retired I was able to spend many hours working on that cottage almost rebuilding the entire cottage to make it adequate for prayer retreats. Many people have donated money to make the renovations possible. Now we have a place at a church camp that is available for anyone who would like to spend 24 to 48 hours alone with God. God is our provider.

Chapter 10

God's Healings

"I am the Lord who heals you."
Exodus 15:26

Little Steve's Eye

Jeremiah 32:17
Ah, Sovereign LORD, you have made the heavens and the earth by your great power and outstretched arm. Nothing is too hard for you.

My youngest brother, Steve, one day walked in front of Dave as he was playing baseball. Dave swung the bat full force just as Steve wandered in front of him. The bat hit Steve in the eye. That horrible event makes me tremble even as I write about it. The scream, the horror, the terror in mom and dad as mom held Steve's head on her lap and his eyeball in the palm of her hand to keep it from dangling out. Dad raced through traffic lights laying on the horn all the way to the hospital.

The doctor was able to stitch his eye back in place and hoped for the best. They wouldn't know for weeks whether he would lose his eyesight. Some weeks later Steve walked behind someone on the swing and was hit in the eye again. This was while his eye was healing and it reopened the wound! More excitement! We had another rush to the hospital. This time however it resulted in a praise session around the dinner table as the doctor had told Mom that there had been a pocket of blood formed behind the eye and the collision with the swing had probably saved his eyesight!! What a lesson that *"all things work together for the good of those who love God."*

A Teen Calling for the Elders

James 5:14
Is any one of you sick? He should call the elders of the church to pray over him and anoint him with oil in the name of the Lord. And the prayer offered in faith will make the sick person well; the Lord will raise him up.

I had the issue of healing come to me rather abruptly when I was a teenager. I had gone to the doctor for a physical. She found strong evidence of diabetes and said, "It appears you have diabetes and that is going to hinder you from being an overseas missionary." I went back home and I talked to my mom and dad about it. At that time my dad was really walking with the Lord, and he said, "Dick, if you really want to be healed, if you really think God has called you to be a missionary, maybe you should call for the elders and have them anoint and pray for you."

I was a 16 year old. I was extremely shy. I had never spoken to an elder in my life. They were scary old guys. I said, "Dad, would you call them for me?" My dad wisely said, "Dick, what does the Scripture say? It says, 'If _you_ are sick, _you_ call for the elders.'"

I thought, "No way!" I really began to wonder whether it was better to stay sick than to call on the elders. I continued to read the Scriptures. The Lord prompted me again. I felt him say, "You are sick. You have a need, and man doesn't have the solution for your need. Call the elders." So, mustering all my courage I called one of the elders. With my hesitancy and nervous voice I said, "This is Dick LaFountain." – "Who?" – "Norman's son. Dick LaFountain." –"Oh yeah, what can I do for you Dick?" "I would like the elders to anoint and pray for me after church on Sunday." Our elders didn't always gather at the front to pray for people. It was only by special appointment. That Sunday came and the elders heard my diagnosis and my sense of being called to be a missionary. They laid hands on me, anointed me with oil, and trusted the Lord with me for my healing.

A week later, the final test came back on the diabetes The doctor said, "I don't know where the diagnosis came from before, but you don't have any evidence of diabetes in your system. You've been completely healed." Isn't that great?! God does wonderful things when we listen to him.

Healing My Weed Poisoning

Psalm 107:20
He sent His word and he healed them,
and delivered them from their destructions.

Back in chapter two I told you about my battle with weed poisoning that afflicted me every year in July. If you've never had poison ivy then you don't know the agony of the itch and running sores.

Marilyn's dad said he never had poison Ivy. He could tear it out by the roots and it wouldn't affect him. When we went to live with them in a big farmhouse before going to the mission field there was a whole slope of poison ivy growing by the pond. Marilyn assumed she was like her dad and never got poison ivy either. One day she took that weed whacker and started attacking it. When she finished she came into the house and showered. The next day her ankles were red and swollen. She had a severe case of poison ivy up to her knees.

I would get what looked like poison ivy, but it was called weed poisoning. It got so bad that I had runny sores all over my body. It would start out as that little blemish then spread. It would spread onto my arms, then to my torso and down to my feet and legs. It would get everywhere. All the parts of my body were infected with this thing.

As I mentioned in chapter two, they took me to the hospital because it was so bad. I actually had blisters all over me that ran with yellow pus that was constantly oozing out of them. Back in that day they didn't have some of the antihistamines and steroid shots like we do today. So they did experiments on me. I was the guinea pig. They put me in these purple baths. I don't know what kind of chemical was in it but they put me in this purple baths to soak. It was supposed to dry up the poison Ivy or the weed poisoning. Well, it didn't. I was in the hospital for a week and it got worse. I had running sores all over my face.

Every year from the time I was eight years old to about sixteen years old, I had that disease every summer and they couldn't do anything about it. Eventually my mother sat down with me and said, "Dick, you said the Lord called you to be a missionary. But if you're missionary, you have to go out in the jungle. You have to go out in the weeds and you always get this weed poisoning. How could you be a missionary?" She wanted me to be a missionary, but she told me I really needed to think this through. Sadly, she said, "Unless the Lord heals you. I don't think you could be a missionary."

Well, I went to prayer. I remember the night I went to prayer on my knees down by my bedside and asked the Lord to do a miracle in my life. It was about this same time that I had rededicated my life to the Lord to be a missionary. "You need to heal me of this disease," I pleaded. "If you have called me then you must equip me to do your will. I ask you in the name of Jesus to heal this body."

The Lord did just that. After that, I would get little spots of poison ivy on me, but never this spreading disease that I had before. Jesus still heals today.

Aimee's Asthma

2 Corinthians 12:8-10
I asked the Lord three times to take it away from me. He answered me, "I am all you need. I give you my loving-favor. My power works best in weak people." I am happy to be weak and have troubles so I can have Christ's power in me. I receive joy when I am weak. I receive joy when people talk against me and make it hard for me and try to hurt me and make trouble for me. I receive joy when all these things come to me because of Christ. For when I am weak, then I am strong.

I don't claim to know all the mysteries of God. William Cowper, a famous hymn writer penned, *"God works in mysterious ways His wonders to perform."* There are times when God answers prayer immediately in dramatic ways, and there are times when it feels like He does not hear our cries at all. It is a great mystery.

I had just begun pastoral ministry in 1972 as pastor of a little church with about 30 people. One of the topics I preached on was the healing that comes in Christ and how we can trust Him for healing of our bodies. At the time our little daughter, Aimee, had chronic asthma. She would often have asthma attacks and not be able to breathe. It would come on suddenly. We'd often have to rush to the hospital with her, not knowing if she'd make it, and really fearing that she was going to stop breathing before we got there. It was not a pleasant situation. It was life-threatening. It was terrifying. She battled these asthma attacks frequently.

We taught Aimee to pray and trust the Lord for her body. We had trusted the Lord for healing many of our sicknesses. I remember one particular night. I had preached on prayer and healing. We went home and as we went to bed, I knelt beside Aimee's bed to pray with her. I reminded her to pray for Grandma and Pop-pop and then I said, "Remember to pray for your asthma too. Let's ask God to heal you." I bowed my head and I said, "You pray first." There was silence. I thought perhaps she didn't hear me, so I said it again, "Aimee, you go ahead and pray. I'll pray afterwards."

Again there was silence. That seemed strange. I opened my eyes and looked at her. My little girl was lying in her bed with tears streaming down her face. I said, "What's the matter?" She said, "Daddy, I don't think Jesus is going to heal my asthma. I don't think God hears me."

Even as I tell this story after all these years my heart breaks. My little Aimee had this terrible disease. She loved the Lord with all her heart and she had cried to Him, but He didn't answer. We had anointed and prayed for her in church and God had not healed her. There she lay in bed despairing of hope saying, "I don't think God hears me because He didn't answer prayer."

After praying with Aimee I went back to our bedroom and shared with Marilyn what Aimee had said. We just wept and prayed. After this I stopped preaching on healing. I was wrestling with the Lord about this whole matter of healing because He hadn't answered our prayer for Aimee.

A Paralyzed Man Is Healed

Isaiah 53:5
But he was pierced through for our transgressions, He was crushed for our iniquities. The chastisement of our peace was upon Him, and with His stripes we are healed.

A few weeks later I received a phone call from a family in the church that had not attended our church for years. They'd been away from the church for about ten years, long before I ever came there. They got mad at somebody in the church, so they quit coming. I had visited them on many occasions trying to encourage them to come back to church.

I remember what they said to me on that first visit. They looked at me and said, "Pastor LaFountain, we don't need to come to church. We have Rex Humbard on the TV and he preaches a lot better than you do." (How would they know? They had never heard me preach.) I said to them, "I don't doubt that he preaches well. But God didn't say listen to good preachers. He said, *"Gather yourselves together and do not forsake it as the manner of some is and do it even more when you see the day of the Lord approaching."* They were stubborn and disobedient people.

That morning I received a phone call from the wife. She was frantic. She said, "Pastor LaFountain, you need to come right now. My husband has had a stroke. He's paralyzed from his neck down and he won't let me call for an ambulance. He said call the preacher."

I wanted to say, "Do you have Rex Humbard's phone number? Call him." But I didn't. I wondered in my mind why they were you calling me. They weren't my parishioners. They were mean spirited people. They were not walking with God. They were disobedient to the Holy Spirit. My daughter hadn't been healed of her disease and loves Jesus with all her heart. What right did they have to ask me to come and pray for them?

I buttoned my lip and didn't say it, but I thought it. She pleaded but I argued, "You need to call an ambulance and get him to the hospital immediately." She countered, "I can't, my husband won't let me. He's paralyzed. He's lying on the floor and he says you've got to call Pastor LaFountain. God said 'Call Pastor La Fountain.'"

I rolled my eyes and I said, "I'll be right over." On the way over to their house I was struggling. I didn't want to pray for this guy. I didn't believe for a moment that God was going to heal him. I really questioned whether God was going to heal anybody and certainly not through me.

I drove to the house but I was struggling with my own lack of faith. As I approached the house the Holy Spirit whispered to me, "Speak to him about his spiritual condition." Then the Lord gave me Hebrews 10:25, *"Forsake not the assembling of yourselves together as the matter of some is."*

I walked in the front door and there he was on the floor. He hadn't moved. He couldn't move, except to turn his neck. He could talk, but he was completely paralyzed. He told me how desperate he was and that he didn't know what to do. The he explained, "Pastor, God told me to call Pastor LaFountain and have him pray for you. Then the Lord said, 'Pastor LaFountain has a word for you. Do you have a word for me?'"

I thought, "Do I ever have a word for you!" I knew that God was in this. Boldly I told him about his sin. I was blunt and I was direct. I told him the word that the Lord spoke to me on the way over to see him. I said, "You are disobedient to the Holy Spirit. You know the word of God. You've disobeyed for ten years. You haven't gathered together with other believers. You're angry at a brother in Christ. You are unforgiving and you are bitter and God is holding that against you. This has been God's judgment on you for your sin." Sometimes I just lose patience with people. I was not merciful with that man. I had no pity him. I told him what God put on my heart.

The guy was still laying on the floor as I said these things. He started to cry. He was under conviction. He said, "You are right. God spoke to my heart about that. That's exactly what God's been saying to me and I'm wrong. I am bitter and angry and I have forsaken the Lord in His house. I need God's forgiveness. Pastor, please pray with me."

So, I prayed with him. He confessed his sins and asked the Lord to forgive him and wash away those sins. When he finished praying he said, "Okay. Pastor, now you can anoint and pray for my healing. Now you can pray for my body."

I wanted to say, "I'm not going to pray for you. You don't deserve it." But the Lord didn't say, "If you deserve it, call for the elders of the church and ask them to pray over you and anoint you with oil." He says do it in the name of the Lord. So, in those moments, I knelt down next to him on the floor, anointed him with oil, and prayed, "Lord Jesus, you are stronger than any disease. You are the God of all of our health and our strength and I ask that if it be your will that you would touch this man and heal his body in Jesus' name. Amen."

My intent was to finish the prayer and then tell the woman to call an ambulance. No sooner had I finished praying when he said, "Wow. Something just happened." Then he moved his arms.

Surprisingly he moved his body. He sat up. From there he got to his knees, then he stood up. He started moving around the room. He did exercises. He got on the floor. This 80 year old guy started doing pushups on the floor! By the time he'd finished, he jumped up and started running around the room shouting, "Hallelujah. Praise the Lord. I am healed."

I was shocked. I thought, "This is not right. My poor little daughter is at home with asthma, with attack after attack. She loves the Lord, pure in heart, simple in faith, not disobedient to God, and here was this son of a gun who in a moment of conviction confesses his sins and the Lord forgives him and the Lord heals him. It's not fair."

Of course I rejoiced with him. It was a miracle. But before I left I told him what he needed to do to complete his repentance, and that was to start going back to church. Well, that brother and his wife showed up for church the next Sunday morning. They were faithful to the forgiveness that God gave them. They followed through and they came to church. But when they saw the other family they had been angry with for ten years all the bitterness came back and they never returned to the church, still he remained healed.

I look at that and I have a thousand questions. I struggled with that for many years. As I preach the word of God it is not with some name it and claim it pie-in-the-sky faith. I do not understand the ways of the Lord, why he heals some and leaves others on their sick beds. I have seen strange things. I have seen wondrous things. I have seen things that just don't make sense to me. I don't want anyone to be discouraged from trusting the Lord for healing. But God is God and does what he pleases in heaven and on earth.

> The Lord says, *"Not by might nor by power*
> *but by my Spirit says the Lord."* (Zechariah 4:6)

Aimee's Broken Arm

Jeremiah 32:27
"I am the Lord, the God of all mankind. Is anything too hard for me?"

It was the last year that we were in Brazil before we came back to the States on our first furlough. Our daughter happened to be roller-skating in the front of our house, which had a nice slope so she could roll down the hill and go near the street, then climb back up and roll down again. Aimee was a wonderful loving little girl, but she was no athlete. Her process of roller-skating was with extreme caution. Unfortunately, she lost her footing, slipped and fell down on her arm and broke it.

I remember the scream. I remember the horror of going outside and seeing my daughter with her arm bent out of shape at a 30 degree angle. You could see her arm was broken and bent in the middle.

Of course the heroic dad that I am, I wanted to help, so I rushed to her side. I knew what to do. I thought it would be best to set it right away. I know now that was a bad idea, but it was the gut reaction of a father wanting to help his daughter. So, I grabbed Aimee's arm and pulled hard on it to try to reset it. It didn't help. It just made matters worse.

We rushed her to the emergency clinic. They took x-rays and then they set the arm properly, and put a cast on it. This was just weeks before leaving to go home to America. They said in six weeks the cast needed come off. "When you get home," they instructed, "have the doctor take it off and check that it was set properly." They were not able to look at that while it was mending itself.

After six weeks of great irritation from wearing a cast Aimee wanted it off. So we carefully removed the cast. We were heartsick. I wanted to cry. I said, "Oh God, what have I done to my baby?" The doctors told us the arm needed to be re-broken and reset. We couldn't bear to put our daughter through that again.

He said, "In two weeks you'll come back and then we'll have to reset it." We prayed. I'll tell you there have never been moments when I've prayed harder. I felt it was my fault, my stupidity that caused this break to be worse than it needed to be. I prayed, "Oh God, we need you to do a miracle for Aimee. We need you to heal this arm so she doesn't have to go through this pain." Our prayer warriors and friends went to the throne and said, "Lord, you're our friend, Jesus. We've walked with you and we've seen you do great things for people that didn't deserve it. Would you heal Aimee's arm?"

Two weeks later we went to the doctor. The doctor unraveled all that gauze and the splint. We looked and her arm was perfect. Not a bend, not a bump. Nothing was wrong. It was perfectly mended! Praise the Lord!

Healing My Mouth Sore

Jeremiah 30:17
*"But I will restore you to health
and heal your wounds, declares the Lord."*

For many months I was suffering. I had a calcium deposit in my mouth that would rub my tongue like sandpaper while I was preaching. I would finish the service with bleeding gums. It was painful. I went to the dentist, then to an oral surgeon. He ground it off and sewed it up. After a week or so, it grew back. It kept scraping on my tongue when I spoke. This went on for months. I was in pain every time I preached. I asked the Lord to heal me. I was doing everything the doctors told me to do, but it just kept coming back.

One of the godly men in our church came up to me after a service and asked, "Pastor Dick, why haven't you called for the elders to come and anoint and pray for you?" I felt that was a rebuke to me. I responded that the Lord hadn't told me to do so, and when He does tell me, I will do it.

Another couple of months went by and I was leading a prayer retreat at a church camp. There were probably about twenty lay people gathered around in a circle and just a few pastors. While we were in the middle of that prayer service, the Lord whispered to my heart, "Now I want you to ask to be anointed and prayed for." I looked around and thought, "Oh, it's mostly lay people. They aren't elders or pastors." But the Lord said now was the time. I told them the story of my calcium deposit and how it was not healed after many months. I said, "I need you to anoint and pray for me." All of them came forward and I knelt down. They prayed for me. Nothing happened.

The next morning I woke up and as I prepared to go to breakfast, I realized there was no pain in my mouth. I could feel no calcium rubbing my tongue. I went to the bathroom, opened my mouth real wide and looked in with a flashlight. That calcium deposit was gone. The redness was gone. The scar tissue was gone. There was no evidence that irritation had ever been there. God had healed me!

So when the Lord tells you that you need to be anointed and prayed for that's him stimulating your faith and saying, "Now is the time."

Healing My Plantar Wart

Proverbs 4:20-22
*My son, give attention to my words, for they are life
to those who find them and health to all their body.*

This particular year I had been struggling with a plantar wart that would not go away. The doctor tried acid, burning it off, and finally surgery to remove the wart. But it kept coming back. It was an odd ailment. I had plantar warts when I was young but rarely as an adult. The fact that it kept coming back seemed very odd.

I was leading a prayer retreat with pastors in the fall of that year. As we were praying, I asked if anyone had a prayer need? We were sitting in a circle and had placed a chair in the middle for anyone to sit in who needed prayer. I humorously called it the "chair of shame," because most people didn't want to be the center of everyone's attention, but really it was the "chair of blessing." Anyone who had a need could come and sit in the chair and be prayed for by the group. What happened next surprised me.

No one came to sit in the chair. The Holy Spirit whispered to me and said, "Why don't you sit in the chair?" I thought, "Me, with all my baggage? No way. I'm not going to tell them my troubles." Still no one came. Finally the Holy Spirit urged me to be a good example and sit in the chair. I thought it might be an opportune time for the men to pray for my plantar wart.

I sat in the chair and one of my pastor friends came up to me and asked, "Dick I want to pray for you but not for your body. I want to know what's hurting in your heart?" That caught me off guard. I thought he was going to pray for my toe, that's what was hurting.

Without thinking about it I opened my mouth to respond and to my surprise I blurted out, "My daddy doesn't love me." Suddenly I started crying. I sobbed, "My daddy has never loved me and never told me he loved me. He never touched me tenderly. He had never affirmed me in any way. Now he's in a nursing home and he is out of his mind and I'll never hear my dad say, "I love you, my son," or "I'm proud of you."

I grew up in a home where I didn't get affirmation. There weren't many positive comments or praise given to any of us. My parents didn't know how to give affirming words because their parents didn't affirm them. No one ever said "I love you" when they were growing up. Nobody ever gave dad any tender touches. There were lots of touches, but they weren't tender. So that lack of positive affirmations passed along through the generations to our family. We too did not get many affirmations. I remember being very insecure about everything.

A few years earlier my dad started exhibiting symptoms of Alzheimer's. He was now in a nursing home and couldn't recognize anyone. We would go in to talk to him. He would just babble incoherently.

This realization caught me off guard. I was shocked. I hadn't been thinking about my dad not loving me, but it must have been deep in my heart. It had been there for years and I hadn't recognized it. I wept as I told my story of an unloving father and the missing affirmation from my dad. Other men identified with my pain. They too had experienced a lack of love from their fathers. They were quietly sobbing in their seats as I spoke. When I finished they gathered around me to pray for me. They laid hands on me and prayed that the Lord would lift that heavy burden and that the Lord would take the bitterness out of my heart and heal it, that this healing would extend to the healing that I needed in my body.

After the prayer retreat I felt the Lord say, "You need to go visit your dad." I argued, "Lord, he's in a nursing home. He doesn't understand anything. He doesn't know anybody." But the Lord continued to say, "Go." As I prepared to go I asked the Lord for a miracle that somehow in my visit my dad would convey to me that he loved me.

A couple weeks later I drove out to Michigan to visit my dad in the nursing home. I found him sitting in his little wheelchair. His head was bowed. There was drool coming from his mouth. I walked in and approached the wheelchair. I knelt down in front of him and I said, "Dad, dad!" He just stared blankly into space as though he didn't hear me. After a few moments he looked toward me and I repeated, "Dad, it's your son. It's Richard. It's Dick. I'm here to visit you."

My dad's eyes suddenly became very clear and focused. He looked at me and smiled. Then he reached out and took my cheek and pinched and shook it lovingly. As he did this he babbled something unintelligible. He was smiling the whole time. I don't think he was speaking in tongues, but I interpreted that expression. I interpreted that as the answer to my prayer. Dad could never say, "I love you" when he was clothed in his right mind. But when he took my cheek I felt him saying, "You're my son, and I'm proud of you." He had never done that before or since.

I took it as God's blessing that dad was still able to say, "I love you. I'm proud of you son." That day the Lord healed my heart. A burden was lifted. I am so glad the Lord healed that wound in my heart that had been there all my life. Had my dad died my heart would have remained wounded. I would have carried my bitterness deep down inside without knowing it for the rest of my life.

I drove back home with peace in my heart that my dad did love me, though his life experience kept him from being able to express it. That night when I went to bed as I took my socks off I thought of my plantar wart. I examined my foot. It was gone. Not even a red mark or a scar was left. God healed my heart and my foot. A year later dad went home to be with the Lord.

Part 3

God Who Equips Me

But you shall receive power when the Holy Spirit has come upon you; and you shall be witnesses to Me in Jerusalem, and in all Judea and Samaria, and to the end of the earth.

Acts 1:8

Chapter 11

God's Authority

"For this purpose the Son of God was manifested, that he might destroy the works of the devil." 1 John 3:8

I have given you authority to trample on snakes and scorpions and to overcome all the power of the enemy; nothing will harm you. Luke 10:19

Martinha and the Devil

James 4:7
Resist the devil and he will flee from you.

We were in Brazil serving as missionaries. Brazil is a spiritist country which means a lot of witchcraft goes on. Eighty percent of the population has dabbled in the occult. We saw a lot of demonic activity in the Brazilian culture.

We were trying to plant a church in a little village in the center of a strong spiritist area. The young pastor leading the church was fighting against the demonic forces and casting out demons whenever necessary.

Living in the middle of Satan's territory had an effect on his family. Evil was like a thick darkness all around them. One night his little five year old daughter woke up screaming. She told her dad there was a monster in the room. She pointed, "He's up in the corner and he keeps looking at me and scaring me." Her dad went into the room thinking she was just having a nightmare. So, he came in the room and he sat down with her on the bed and assured her there was no little monster in the corner. He told her that she knows Jesus as her Savior and he would protect her. He talked and comforted her for ten minutes or so. Wanting to go back to bed he asked her to look up in the corner to see if there was still something there. She looked up in the corner and screamed, "Daddy, it's still there! That little creature is still up in there staring at me! It's mean it's going to come and get me. Make him go away!"

Her father thought it strange that she was now wide awake, but still seeing this evil thing. So he suggested they sing some songs they had learned in Sunday School. They rejoiced in the Lord singing a number of choruses. Another 15 or 20 minutes passed. Again he said, "Okay, honey. Look up in the corner. She looked up again and in terror cried, "No, daddy, he's still there and he's even bigger! It's coming after me, daddy help me." Later he told me he didn't know what to do. He said they don't teach this kind of stuff in Bible schools and seminaries. Finally, after praying again, he turned to Martha and asked, "Martha, what scripture verses did you learn in Sunday School? Let's quote them together.'

She had learned Matthew 19:14 and began to quote it with authority:

> "Suffer the little children to come unto me and forbid them not for such is the kingdom of heaven."

As she uttered those words, *"Suffer the little children to come unto me and forbid them not for such is the kingdom of heaven,"* there was an audible pop in the room, like a balloon exploding. Her father heard it. She heard it. They both looked up in the corner and Martha shouted, "It's gone, daddy, it's gone! Thank God it's gone. The evil monster is gone."

Her father walked away from that situation amazed and discovered something new. Demons can torment children. Demons can attack Christians, trying to intimidate them. Even little children are susceptible to the enemy's attacks. That evil spirit was pestering and trying to gain access to her room and to her life. Even so, she could talk, quote scripture, pray and sing, but what made the enemy flee was the authority with which she stood on the word of God.

Jose Luiz Finds Freedom

1 John 2:14
I have written to you, fathers, Because you have known Him who is from the beginning... young men, Because you are strong, and the word of God abides in you, And you have overcome the wicked one.

Let me tell you the story of a twelve year old boy, one of our first converts to Christ in Brazil. Jose grew up in a spiritist home. His parents were nominal Catholics but they also, like most people in Brazil, practiced various forms of witchcraft to protect their loved ones. Jose even as a young boy hated the spiritist practices of offering sacrifices or grain or a strangled chicken left at an intersection to turn away evil. He hated it. He knew it was wrong to try to appease evil with evil. He had experienced many night terrors because of it.

In the darkness of their wooden shack in a poor village he lay panic stricken, clutching his ragged night clothes, trembling, sweating, and cringing from the unseen evil he sensed haunting his room. His eyes scoured the night searching for some ray of hope in his chamber of fear. His eyes scanned hopelessly the pictures of saints and fictitious spiritist guides which were to protect him. Even their faces seemed to turn into horrid ghouls grinning and taunting him. His hands trembled and fumbled for the charm bracelets of witchcraft in which so many trusted, but in his little hands they appeared to be chains tightening about him and shackling him to his fears. He screamed, throwing the fetishes across the room and burying his head deep in his pillow he sobbed, "Is there no one who can save me from this hell?"

His parents tried to help. His fears kept him awake so many nights they worried that his health would soon break down. They took him to doctors, to psychologists, to therapists, but they seemed as puzzled as the boy to find a cure for his chronic fear. Year after year his fears multiplied and his nights became dreaded battlegrounds.

"It must be spiritual," his parents reasoned. "Perhaps an evil spirit has a hold on him. He will need to receive other good spirits to fight it off." They forcibly dragged him to the spiritist practitioners for help. First they prescribed several incantations and more bracelets, then a sacrifice of grain and candles to be left on a street corner at midnight to ward off the evil spirits. Still his fears remained. A blood sacrifice would be necessary to more powerfully appease the spirits. A chicken must be offered and left in the streets for the spirits to devour. Yet his fears remained. His parents had spent all they had to pay for such incantations, but seemingly to no avail. A final effort must be made at any cost. He must surrender his will to the will of the spirits and receive spirit guides to enable him to overcome this evil. He must be baptized in blood!

The costly sacrifice of a goat was made. He was locked in a shed in the back of the spiritist center where blood was poured over his head until it soaked his entire body. Then he was forced to remain sitting on the ground for three days, locked in a dark room, waiting for the spirit guides to enter. When he left the room, the spirit guides had manifested themselves and Jose left with an eyen greater fear of spiritism than he had of the dark. His fear of the dark continued. Sleepless nights were the norm. A light had to be left burning all night for him to get any sleep.

As he grew older, so did his hatred for the spiritist rites, for deep within he knew that they were cohorts with his fears. Then one day he heard of Jesus. Not the Jesus the priests spoke of, and not the Jesus the spiritists acknowledged, but the Jesus of the Bible, the loving, healing, living Jesus who brought peace.

It happened by accident. He was recovering from two broken legs he had received in a terrible bus accident. His parents had dragged him to those horrible spiritist centers offering sacrifices in hopes of healing him. He abhorred it all and tried to get away from home as much as possible. That is when it happened. He was hobbling on his crutches one Sunday afternoon, sulking in his misery when he saw other children running past him with smiles on their faces. "Where are you going?" he shouted. "The missionary is here! The missionary is here! At the school, come on," they shouted. So he did, just out of curiosity, of course. It was curious indeed. The missionary used puppets, taught songs and Bible verses, and told stories with his funny accent.

He could not help but laugh. But something else struck him profoundly. It was that Wordless Book that told of God's love, our sin, Jesus' death on a cruel cross, and how we could have a clean heart and peace with God. It was as if someone had turned on a bright light and he could see there was hope for his fears. He would come back. He must hear more!

He did return. Every Sunday he went to the school to hear the missionary. He found it in his thoughts all week long. Soon he was going to the missionary's little church too. This was great. It was what he always longed for. Finally, Jose realized that going to church was not enough to calm his fears. Jesus wanted to come into his life and live with him. One night, when the missionary gave the invitation, he prayed and asked Jesus to be his Savior. There was no dramatic happening, but just a new peace and joy knowing that Jesus was now the conqueror of all his fears.

Immediately Jose was interested in studying the Bible. He took home and soon finished all the studies we could give him. He began the Theological Education by Extension program and did very well. When challenged to do a memory contest he memorized 80 verses in two months! He brought his friends and family to church too to hear of Jesus.

Yet, as time went by we could tell that there was a problem. Jose could never pray out loud. At first we thought it was timidity, but even the most timid in the group could voice a simple prayer, but not Jose. When we'd give a time for prayer at a youth meeting, though everyone else would pray, he would remain silent. Once I thought I could trap him into praying. He was taking up the offering and when he came to the pulpit with it, I publicly called on him to ask God's blessing on it. The silence of the moment spoke loudly of his problem. I waited, but he stood squirming, agonizing, yet not a word did he even mumble. I had to ask someone else to pray.

The situation finally came to a head one day. Jose was in the church listening to Christian music as he often did. I was outside dealing with a spiritist man, a man possessed by demons. When I walked back into the sanctuary, the Holy Spirit prompted me to ask Jose if he had been involved in spiritism. (Up to this time I knew little of his life story.) He looked up at me shocked and said, "Why do you ask?" I related that I had just spoken to a spiritist and the Holy Spirit prompted me to ask. He walked over to the cassette tape player and turned it off. I knew then I had touched on a sore spot, he never willingly turned off the music. He said, "Pastor, let's talk. It's a long story."

He proceeded to describe to me his childhood fears and his involvement in spiritism with all the terrifying details. I began to understand his inability to pray. I had been reading about spiritism and demon possession and had discovered the true meaning of "baixar no chao", the blood baptism ceremony. It was a total surrender of one's life and mind and soul to the occult. It was a selling of one's soul to the devil! This, of course, brings about captivity to Satan and occult oppression or possession, depending on the individual case. Jose, even though a Christian, was chained to the past by that blood sacrifice in which his parents sold his soul. The devil was refusing to let go, and gradually tightening the chains of his usurped ownership.

I shared with him the meaning of blood sacrifices, what happened to him in the spiritual realm when he surrendered to the occult. Then with scripture I shared how wonderfully Christ has set us free by his blood and broken all the covenants left standing, that we by the exercise of our faith in Jesus and by the word of our testimony, must break those bonds of Satan's claims and rebuke him, his efforts, his allegiance, and his parent's allegiance once and for all.

That afternoon, standing at the front of a little wooden plank floored chapel, leaning over the pulpit, Jose said, "I want to pray now." With tears rolling down his face he confessed Jesus as the only Lord of his life and in prayer broke every covenant with Satan. He was finally free – totally and visibly free, to serve Jesus. The changes weren't immediate but Jose began to blossom. He could pray!

Dona Iris, Freed From Bondage

Luke 10:19
*I have given you authority to trample on snakes and scorpions
and to overcome all the power of the enemy; nothing will harm you.*

The complete story of Dona Iris I cannot tell because we were not directly involved with her over a long period of time. But we were acquainted with her from the work in Jardim das Palmeiras in Porto Alegre. Dona Iris came to Porto Alegre from the city of Belo Horizonte, where she was raised. Her husband worked with marble cutting and the work possibilities are what drew him to the south. Dona Iris had been an influential leader in spiritism in Belo and was well known for her powers. She had attained to the position of "*Mãe-de-santo*" which is, "mother of saints", so designated because she was a priestess of *Umbanda* and could contact the spirit world. In other words she was a very powerful medium to communicate with spirits who communicated through her.

She rarely spoke specifically of her exploits because at the time of her mediumship, she entered into a trance and could remember nothing from when she was in that state. She only heard of her own exploits from others who accompanied her and were eye witnesses. They had related that at the midnight services in which they were to go to a cemetery as a group to offer sacrifices, perform rituals, etc. she would approach the chained and locked gates, go into a trance, and by some amazing feat would pass through the gates and lead them into the cemetery.

Dona Iris first came in contact with the Gospel when her neighbor, the Jardim das Palmeiras pastor's mother, invited her to a Bible study in her home. Iris attended and listened, carefully asking questions. It was the first time she had ever heard the message of God's love and salvation through faith in him. When the pastor asked if anyone wanted to receive Christ, she was one of the first to raise her hand. She prayed the sinner's prayer and received Christ as her Savior. Immediately she began attending the Alliance Church and learned more about Christ. Her questions were many and sincere, even though often difficult to answer, because her entire orientation throughout life had been spiritist. Many of her questions were reflective ones. Learning a new Bible truth she would question, "Why do the spiritists say...(such and such)?"

The oddity in her story is that there was no power encounter, as one would expect when a medium comes to Christ. The struggle seemed to be a physical one, wherein she was sickly from the time she became a Christian. The only experience of "deliverance" as one would expect, came after church one evening. She had been feeling down and ill for some time and doubts were plaguing her mind. For some unknown reason, after church she was overpowered by something and began writhing and struggling as if in a wrestling match. The evil spirit spoke out and claimed her to be his possession.

The young pastor was startled by all this and began to pray, pleading the blood of Jesus, and rebuking the evil spirit. Her condition worsened as she was being overpowered and the evil spirit would not leave. At that point a young Chilean woman, recently converted, stepped up to her and putting her hands on Dona Iris, rebuked the evil spirit in Jesus' name and told him to get out. Immediately the evil spirit left her and she returned to her normal state. We do not understand all of this or why her case seemed so different, but in any event, she was delivered and by a mere child in the faith who didn't stand there trembling with fear, but in simple faith commanded the situation as she knew we have the right to do.

How often we shake and tremble in fear at such manifestations of evil spirits, but Paul exhorts the Philippians (1:28) *"In nothing terrified by your adversaries."* We must recognize our safety in Christ and our position with him. Jesus said, *"I give you authority over all the powers of the enemy; and nothing shall by any means hurt you."*

Delivered from Demon Possession

Mark 5:9
Then Jesus asked him, "What is your name?"
"My name is Legion," he replied, "for we are many."

Working in the little village of Vila Elsa had been a real battleground for many months. These last few months had been very discouraging. One of our new believers had been forbidden to attend our services by her husband. Another had become depressed and attempted suicide on several occasions. Another teenager had been hospitalized in serious condition with a strange skin infection which covered his body. Another recent convert denied her faith.

We had a wonderful deliverance ministry of a man who was a warlock (a male witch) and a medium. Alair received the Gospel of John we had distributed house to house and loved what he read. It was strange when he showed up at the church. The service was already in session and we were worshiping. As he walked in the door suddenly everyone got quiet. He came in with his dog as well, which is not unusual in this little village.

As we were concluding the service and serving communion I began to serve the grape juice and speak of the blood of Jesus. Immediately his dog stood up and ran forward growling and snarling and showing its teeth at me. It was a strange experience, almost a physical attack.

After the service I asked Delfino, our lay pastor, who that man was and why everybody got quiet. It seemed everyone knew Alair. He told me that Alair was a powerful spiritist warlock for the whole northern part *of Porto Alegre. He was a Pai de Santo, (father of saints) a priest of Umbanda* and *Candomble*, a medium and the head of spiritism and black magic for thousands of people in the northern region of Porto Alegre.

Alair came back to church several times. After every service he would tell me that he received the Gospel of John and read it all the way through. He said he loved reading it. He loved hearing about Jesus. He wanted to thank us for giving him the Bible. But each time I would try to tell him about Jesus, he would get nervous and irritated.

One day as I stood by my car speaking with him I determined to clearly present Christ to him and invite him to receive Christ. As soon as I started speaking about Jesus he became angry and agitated. I was determined to pray over him whether he liked it or not. So, without his consent, I started to pray. At that point he actually took his fist and smashed into the side of my car, denting it.

On another occasion he came by the church again and talked to me about loving the Bible he had received. I told him that it was nice that he liked the Bible but he needed Jesus. He said he wanted to to receive Jesus, but each time I talked to him about Jesus he would get angry and he didn't know why.

That night the youth service was over so we put everyone out of the church and asked Alair to come into the church to pray with us. Steve Renicks, my missionary colleague, and I did this because we believed that there was going to be a demonic encounter and we didn't want our young people influenced by it.

For two and a half hours we talked, shared Christ, prayed, pled the blood of Jesus, and claimed the victory in Jesus' name, all to no avail. Each time we would tell Alair that he needed Jesus he would begin to pray then would gag and choke, fall on the flood, and writhe in pain. At times he would lose control of himself and became violent. He couldn't hurt us or release himself from the circle of prayer (we held our hands around him as we prayed). Though he was a strong 36 year old man he couldn't break our hold. Finally, after one particularly difficult demonic outburst, he passed out on the floor.

Twice more he raged overturning pews and smashing the pulpit. Then he'd awaken from passing out and would ask what happened. We told him that he was trying to pray, but demons would not let him. We told him that the demons he had received in spiritism and witchcraft could not stop him from receiving Christ as his Savior because demons could not block his will.

We were exhausted. We wanted to be done with this ugly business. At one point Alair managed to pray confessing his sins. We were overjoyed by this. I remember Steve saying, "Good! We're done here! Let's go home." But I sensed he wasn't free at all. Then the Holy Spirit prompted me to tell Alair to not only confess his sins, but invite Jesus to come into his heart. He tried over and over again, but couldn't get the words out, as he would gag, choke, become violent and then pass out.

Finally, in exhaustion, Steve and I didn't know what to do. We had tried everything we knew how to do. They don't teach you this stuff in Bible School or seminary. So we picked up a hymnal while Alair raged and we began to sing praises. As we sang Alair melted to his knees in front of the cross that was hanging on the wall.

This time he came back to his senses very upset that someone broke the church furniture. We again told him what was going on, and again he said he really, really wanted to receive Jesus. This time, however, when he prayed he started to choke, but forced the words out, "Jesus... come...into... my...heart..." As soon as he said, "Come into my heart" he suddenly burst into joyful tears, confessing his sins and praising God for his forgiveness. He was free!!!

Edu & Jandira Released from Bondage

Matthew 28:18
*Jesus came and spoke unto them, saying,
All power is given unto me in heaven and in earth.*

Edu and Jandira got saved in a home visit. After a few weeks of discipleship they decided to burn all their fetishes and things that belonged to spiritism and witchcraft. They were terrified about doing this. Edu, a tall, gentle, very black semi-literate man with a deep voice said he was afraid, "I'll go down" meaning he'd be overpowered by demons that would make him pass out. We encouraged them that the Lord was stronger than demons and we would be there with other believers to pray for them. We planned a fetish burning service in the church front yard the following Sunday.

We were really concerned about this because our congregation was very small. Most people were new believers. We prayed and asked the Lord to stand with us as they took this huge step of faith. Normally our attendance was around 40 people. That night as we waited for the service to start little by little people began to trickle into the church. No one knew that this burning of fetishes was going to take place because we had no way of telling them. But God was calling people together on that special night. I was surprised to see that people came from the other side of the city traveling by bus an hour and a half to get there, because God told them they needed to be there. That night we had 63 people gathered together in a large circle around a huge bonfire in which the fetishes were burned. An odd thing happened as we started to burn those fetishes.

First, we doused all of them with alcohol. Alcohol is very flammable but safe. And then we lit matches and threw them on the alcohol. But the alcohol wouldn't ignite. We tried three times. Then we prayed and asked the Lord for help. This time the alcohol ignited and the fetishes burned with a huge plume of black smoke. As we did so we sang, prayed and held hands in a circle. Edu did not "go down." That night they were delivered from the power of Satan's kingdom.

Their daughter, Carmen, attended with them that night and when she saw what God had done, she confessed Christ as her Savior and brought her fetishes to be burned. They remained faithful in the Alliance Church until the last few years when they changed churches. We were not in Porto Alegre when Edu died, but here is the story we were told.

He was in the hospital (I think he had suffered a stroke). One day he looked at Jandira and said' "Honey, I want you to bring my suit to me." Jandira asked why and he told her that he was going to a banquet. She said, "Edu, you are not going to a banquet without me" and he responded, "This time I am." She brought him his suit and put it on him. Sometime later, Edu raised his hands in the air and said, "The angels have come to get me." He dropped his hands and died. Talk about the Lord preparing him for his home going! What a wonderful way to enter the presence of God.

Mr. Andre Walks Away

Matthew 13:7-8
But when the sun rose, the seeds were scorched, and they withered because they had no root. Other seed fell among thorns, which grew up and choked the seedlings. Still other seed fell on good soil and produced a crop—a hundredfold, sixtyfold, or thirtyfold.

Seu Andre (as they called him, Mr. Andrew as we would say) was a big man with n protruding stomach that sagged some inches below his belt buckle. He walked slowly for a man of his age, as if he always had sore feet, from prolonged gout. His wide face seemed generously creased with wrinkles from years of frowning. His cheeks sagged and he always appeared to be chewing, or at the least hiding something in his mouth. His speech was slurred through yellow-stained teeth due to years of chewing tobacco. He was a *gaucho*, the rugged masculine prototype of the pioneer cowboy of southern Brazil. His accent, his habits, his walk, his mannerisms and his attitudes all betrayed that he was long reared in the deep interior of the State and steeped in *gaucho* traditions. He had come to the big city of Porto Alegre, the capital of the south, to establish himself in some business earlier in life. But in his typical manner he refused to break any of the *gaucho* lifestyles that he had developed in his beloved town of Caçapava. His every greeting made the new acquaintance acutely aware of his heritage and he made it a conspicuous point of introducing himself as "Seu Andre, of Caçapava," not a native of this city, only a resident, a passer through, who soon proposed to return to the land of real men.

How Seu Andre came in contact with the Alliance church in Jardim das Palmeiras was a casual happenstance in his search for healing of a long-term ailment. He made it clear that the "missionary" (or divine healer) who cured his ailments would certainly have his respect and allegiance. It was through a simple black spinster with a worse speech impediment than his that he first heard of the Alliance. (She had become a Christian despite her strongly antagonistic spiritist mother, but that's another story.)

While cleaning his home one day, she mentioned the fact that her church believed in divine healing. He had no respect or time for such "blacks" in the true spirit of *gaucho* machismo and racial prejudice, but the healing question deserved investigation. He would at least hear what these evangelicals had to say and see if they had the power to heal his afflictions.

For several months he frequented the services when he felt like it. His wife, a staunch Catholic, followed along giving lip service to the Gospel, but making it quite clear she needed nothing more. She was a Christian Catholic and certainly a better person than any in the church. Andre remained callous to the Gospel and was obviously interested in being healed more than in becoming a Christian. Or could it have been that he wanted more proof of the claims of Christ? After all, Brazil is full of religions and cults, all of them claiming to be the truth. What makes Christianity any different?

One night Andre dreamed of a great chasm between two mountains and an airplane, passing overhead that had engine trouble and went crashing into the rocks below. He awoke and thought nothing more of the dream. The following day, a missionary still in language school came to the church and was to be the speaker. Andre went as usual, speaking to the new missionary and everyone else of his desire to be healed of his gout. The service was quite normal and he enjoyed the lively music and the accordion accompaniment.

When the new missionary stepped to the platform and began in his faltering speech, Seu Andre settled himself back in his seat expecting at most to have a humorous time listening to this foreigner err in his Portuguese, and perhaps to be able to get a quick nap.

But the missionary did the unusual. He used an illustrated message and unfolded a large poster on which there was a picture of a plane flying through treacherous mountains. Andre jumped to the edge of his seat to see more clearly. It was the exact picture of what he had seen in his dream. As the missionary spoke, Andre grabbed at every word, realizing for the first time his separation from God and the necessity of the Savior, or else face certain death and eternal damnation. Tears welled up in his eyes. When the missionary closed the sermon and gave the invitation Andre was already shuffling down the wood plank floor to give his heart to Jesus. He told them of his dream and how fearful it had made him of dying. He cried out for mercy to be saved and recognized Jesus as his only Savior who could deliver his soul from death and give him peace.

Now he spoke of the church as his church. He was a Christian. He forced his wife to go with him and all but pushed her down the aisle each time an invitation was given. But she resisted stubbornly insisting on her own good deeds as proof of her genuine Catholic Christianity. Seu Andre became even more ardent in his pursuit of healing for his gout ridden legs, since now he was a Christian. Surely, God would work this miracle for him.

My meeting with Seu Andre came just after I was appointed to serve in Porto Alegre, but before I had finished language school. I was invited to be the officiating ordained minister at his baptism. Since no one in the church had room for visitors, I stayed in his home for three days. He was eager to please the missionary and perhaps this one would be able to heal his legs.

This was my first experience actually being cut off from English and having no one to help fill in where I lacked knowledge of the Portuguese language. Their hospitality was exceptional, treating me as royalty, serving me the most delicious delicacies of their cuisine, and standing close alongside me watching my every reaction to the strange new tastes, waiting for my first words of praise. Often it was all I could do to smile and say it was good, as I gagged to make it go down. Since I liked it so well, Mrs. Andre heaped another serving onto my plate, to be sure I had enough and watched carefully to see if I downed it all. If I was unable to clean it up, she eyed me suspiciously, saying, "You didn't really like it, did you?" I responded politely that it was good, but I was full. "Well, why didn't you say so," she retorted, "I'll just save you a plateful for later!" How often I was tempted to retreat to the bathroom or outside with the hope that I'd get sick and regurgitate it all. At least the bathroom was a comforting solitude from this island paradise on which I was stranded.

Throughout those days they pumped me with questions about Christianity, the Bible, the church, and America. I had the impression that to them, those four things were inseparably intertwined, and to become a Christian was somehow to become an American ally. (Many Brazilians believe evangelical Christianity or Protestantism to be an American product, a religion invented by Americans.)

While speaking to the question of divine healing and God's will, I mentioned in passing that our daughter Aimee had asthmatic bronchitis and although she had prayed, trusted and been anointed for healing, God in His sovereignty had not seen fit to heal her yet. Andre could not conceive of such a thing and instead of being edified by this example, he pitied me. This poor ignorant suffering American missionary didn't know the cure for asthma. He hurried to his room saying he had the cure for Aimee. A few minutes later he returned with a typewritten sheet and declared in his wrinkled grin, "Here is how to rid her of asthma. I guarantee it. It worked for my son." I took the piece of paper and read it slowly in my imperfect Portuguese. Here is what it said:

Cure for Asthma

If thou art plagued with Asthma
In the secret of thy closet
Prepare thyself a vessel.
Half full of milk you should fill it
Upon the first full moon
Thou shalt make thy way stealthily
to the nearest fig tree
(Be sure no eyes see thee)
There at the foot of the fig tree
Bury the bottle bottom side up
(So as to drain it completely).

Thence thou shalt say these words:
"Away with thee oh asthma
Away with thee forever
As this milk that disappears
So shalt thou ne'er reappear
In the name of Jesus Christ our Savior,
God the Father. Son and the Holy Ghost,
And the blessed Virgin Mary. Amen."

Do this for three consecutive nights with seven "Hail Marys" and your asthma will be gone.

I immediately responded that I could not do something like this because it is non-Biblical and un-Christian and it was clearly a spiritist magical incantation. He became very indignant and said he would not do something spiritist either. He was a Christian. Then he pointed out that it used Jesus' name, just as any of our prayers. "It can't be wrong, it's done in Jesus' name, and after all, the padre (the Catholic priest) was the one who gave it to me!" I insisted on it being nothing like anything we find in the Bible for healing and it was more like superstitious magic. He refused to see it as anything but God given and I heard him mumble as he walked away. "What does a young preacher like you know anyway, it worked didn't it?"

Shortly after moving to Porto Alegre the church received a mission loan of $12,000 to purchase land in a more visible location. (They had been meeting in a back yard where a plywood portable chapel had been built.) The church was facing serious financial difficulties and needed to have each member tithing. The lay pastor asked me to come and preach on tithing in relation to the church's needs because he felt if he would speak on the subject they would misunderstand his motives. I did so laying out clearly the Biblical command and promises for tithers and the national church's statement on it and the obvious necessity of the church. Seu Andre took this as a personal offense since he was dead set against giving regularly to the church.

From there he left the church and moved. The last we heard he had turned spiritist, seeking again the cure for his gout from Satanic sources.

*As when a dog goes to his own vomit,
and becomes abominable, so is a fool who
returns in his wickedness to his own sin.*
Proverbs 26:11 & 2 Peter 2:2

Chapter 12

God's Deliverance

"For this purpose the Son of God was manifested, that he might destroy the works of the devil."
1 John 3:8

I have given you authority to trample on snakes and scorpions and to overcome all the power of the enemy; nothing will harm you.
Luke 10:19

A Teen's Psychic Bondage

Acts 16:16-24
*We met a slave girl who had a spirit of fortune-telling
and who had brought her owners a great deal of money
by predicting the future.*

I was preaching on a Sunday evening and in doing so I felt a tremendous oppression. I had difficulty with the flow of the message as though there was something standing in front of me hindering me, maybe even opposing me. Whenever this has happened in the past it had been that someone was demonized or under the power of the occult and thereby hindering the Holy Spirit in the service. So, I stopped mid-message and paused for a full minute. That usually gets people's attention.

I told them what I felt was going on and I read a long list of occult activities that lead to demon infestation. I said, "Somebody here has dabbled in the occult. I am going to pray and bind the enemy in Jesus' name." I prayed and went on with the sermon.

When I finished preaching almost everyone left except for this one young lady. She came up to me and said, "It's me." I had already put the matter of a hindering spirit behind me so I didn't know what she meant. I asked, "What do you mean, 'It's me?' What are you talking about?" She replied, "I'm the one that has dabbled in the occult." She went on to tell me that her mother regularly went to a psychic. Her mother had given her a note from a psychic which she was told to carry in her purse. It was supposed to protect her from all the diseases and physical afflictions she was experiencing. The note was an incantation. It was supposed to stop the evil and she would have no more sickness. She then reached into her purse and brought out the note. I read it and was appalled. This was just like the Brazilian white magic and demonic spells used that we encountered in Brazil. I couldn't believe this was in an evangelical church in the States.

After I read the note I told her she needed to repent of that witchcraft and turn to the Lord for her body and health. I instructed concerning the Scriptures in Deuteronomy 7:25-26 regarding witchcraft that tell us all items belonging to the devil should be burned to utterly destroy them. It was quite frightening for me to realize that even believers can be deceived into witchcraft as good magic.

I would like to report that she trusted the Lord, but she did not. She continued to be influenced by her psychic mother and she continued to battle undiagnosed illnesses. A few years later I heard that she had died of an unknown illness.

Over the years while working with people involved in the occult and witchcraft I found that it was best to open the Bible and allow them to read God's condemnation of those activities and what should be done about it. I keep these references in the back of my Bible so I can easily find them. I have the individual read it out loud. The effect is powerful. They usually turn white with fear and start to tremble.

I recommend in today's culture that all God's children should have these passages marked in their Bible to use in such occasions.

- **Leviticus 19:26, 31, 20:6, 20:27**
- **Deuteronomy 7:25-26, 18:19-12, 28:15-47**
- **Isaiah 8:19-22, 19:2-3, 47:9-15**
- **Micah 5:12-15**
- **Galatians 5:19**
- **Revelation 21:8**
- **1 Corinthians 10:19-21**
- **2 Corinthians 6:14-17**

Comatose People

In several cases in Brazil and here in the USA I have been called upon to visit someone who was comatose from demonic involvement. Once in Brazil it was a young lady who had been comatose for three days, unable to wake up. No medicines or psychological therapies helped. When I was called I recognized it immediately as an occult phenomenon where a demon caused them to fall under a spell. Another occasion was in New Jersey. A man in my church told me his college age daughter was comatose for three days and would not come out of it.

In each case I did the same thing. I sat by their side and talked to them. They could hear me, just as many people in a coma can hear. They were just unable to respond. I told them what I believed was happening, that they had opened a door for Satan to afflict them through immoral living or occult involvement. I tell them that Jesus came to destroy the work of the devil. Then I opened my Bible and read aloud Psalm 91. It worked EVERY TIME. Before I got finished reading they woke up and asked what was happening. I then shared the Gospel with them and how they could call on the name of the Lord and be saved. I recommend this to anyone dealing with demon possessed, oppressed, or obsessed.

An Affluent Executive

Acts 19:18-20
Many of those who believed now came and openly confessed what they had done. A number who had practiced sorcery brought their scrolls together and burned them publicly. When they calculated the value of the scrolls, the total came to fifty thousand drachmas. In this way the word of the Lord spread widely and grew in power.

This story happened in the United States, so we know these demonic activities and spiritual oppressions happen here as well. I was pastoring in New Jersey in a middle class American town. It was an upper middle class neighborhood with people living in a nice community. My neighboring pastor called me one day to ask me to visit a man of his church who believed his house was haunted. He said, "Dick, I need you to come over. You've been in Brazil, you know about witchcraft and haunted houses and all that stuff. I've got a guy in my church who thinks his house is haunted." He went on to tell me that the man's son had been sick. They had been to every doctor and nothing could make the boy better. He also said they had been hearing noises and seeing things in the house, like someone walking around at night. The man was terrified that it was a ghost. So, this pastor wanted me to come over to convince his parishioner that his house wasn't haunted. I paused for a moment for effect. Then I said, "Well, Dennis, I'll come over, but I'm not going to convince him that his house isn't haunted, because HIS HOUSE IS HAUNTED!"

I went on to explain that if they were seeing things in the dark and hearing noises of people walking through the house at night it is always because somebody had dabbled in the occult. They have been involved with witchcraft in some shape or form.

Dennis assured me this was an upper middle class guy. He had a great job. He was highly educated. He was an executive in a big firm. He was a former Catholic. He was a new Christian. There was no way that he dabbled in the occult. I responded, "I'm just telling you what I know. Let me come over and talk with him."

That evening Dennis and I went over to his lovely home. We sat down and started to chat. I asked him to tell me a little about himself and his background. He told me about his son having tremors and night fears and was seeing things in the dark and hearing bumps in the night like footprints in the house. I just waited for him to finish the story.

"Let me ask you a question," I said, "Have you or anyone in your family dabbled in the occult?" Then I explained what that meant. I identified things like horoscopes, Ouija boards, tarot cards, palm readers, fortune tellers, ESP, psychics and psychic healers and such. I went through a whole litany of things that are spiritual and occult and that God says are an abomination. I explained that they are gateways to demonic activity, and haunted houses are just a symptom of demonic activity.

You could see his face turn red with embarrassment as I spoke. Then the blood drained out of his face. I looked at Dennis and just raised my eyebrows. Even his wife noticed his discomfort and guilt and asked him what it was.

Then he told me his story. He explained, "My son has been sick for months. We have tried everything medically speaking and nothing worked. We've gone to church and they prayed for him and nothing happened. So, I saw this lady advertised in the newspaper. She's called the *"Mother of Saints."* He continued to explain that he decided since nothing worked he was going to call her and see if there was anything she could do. She was based in Texas. He called and asked for her help. She told him there were some things she could do, but there was also something he would have to do in return. She began to send him amulets and items that were supposed to protect his house and family. They were pictures, chains, incantations, cloths, even crosses. He was to put them in strategic places around the house and bury some of them in the backyard. Still with all this his son was not getting better.

Finally, she said the curse on them must be strong. She wanted him to buy a Rolex watch. She specified the make and model number. She wanted him to buy one that cost more than $5,000. She instructed him not to tell his wife or anyone else but keep it a secret. Once he bought the watch he was to send it to her by FedEx. She promised to take the watch and say certain prayers over it. Then she would turn back the hand of the clock and his son would be healed.

The man felt like a fool. He pleaded, "I didn't know it was wrong. She is a Catholic lady. She said prayers in Jesus' name. She used crosses and quoted the Bible. His wife looked at him when he admitted he bought a $5,000 watch and yelled, "You did what? Are you out of your mind?" and they started to argue.

Dennis, the pastor, didn't know about any of this. He sat there dumbfounded. He whispered to me, "I can't believe this. This is a guy in my church dabbling in the occult and getting really deeply into it."

I interrupted their heated argument. I said, "You know there is a solution. You need to repent and ask God's forgiveness. You did it in ignorance. You didn't know that was wrong, but God says it's wrong. I opened the

Scripture, showed him where it says it's wrong. I had him read it out loud from Deuteronomy 7:25-26. I told him he needed to take these things that belong to Satan and burn them so no one else could be entangled in them. After that we were going to walk through every room and claim the victory of Christ over his son, his family, and his house. They were broken and willing.

They walked around the rooms and started collecting things from Satan's kingdom. They had three bags full of all the paraphernalia from this lady. Then he said, pastor, there are things buried in the backyard. I don't know if I can ever find them. I assured him that it was good enough to burn what he could find. Later the Lord would show him where to find those other hidden things and he could burn them.

We spent that evening burning all those things and claiming the victory of Christ over his family. Then we walked through every room of the house claiming Psalm 91 and the protection of the Lord upon that household.

I got a call two weeks later and he said his son had been healed. His son was well for the first time in years. There were no more bumps in the night. There were no footsteps walking through the house and nobody was seeing any ghosts anymore. His house had been set free.

How were they set free? By the word of God and prayer! It's an amazing story. I hope that makes you feel the willies too because there are a lot of Christians who are carelessly dabbling in cultic things. They don't realize that the word of God gives us power over all the work of the enemy. If we repent and surrender those things to the Lord and obey His word, He will put a stop to the enemy's actions.

The rest of the story is that this man was so distraught and upset by being deceived that he got in touch with the FBI through a friend in Texas and made a formal complaint against the lady. The police had already accumulated other complaints against her so they raided her home and found hundreds of thousands of dollars worth of merchandise and cash she had deceived people into sending her. She was arrested and jailed. He received the Rolex watch in return. The Lord returned all that the devil had stolen!

Demonized With Pain

Luke 13:10-13
Now He was teaching in one of the synagogues on the Sabbath. And behold, there was a woman who had a spirit of infirmity eighteen years, and was bent over and could in no way raise herself up. But when Jesus saw her, He called her to Him and said to her, "Woman, you are loosed from your infirmity." And He laid His hands on her, and immediately she was made straight, and glorified God.

I was pastoring a church of 300-400 people. It was a great church but it was filled with conflict from the first day I set foot in it. The complaining and criticizing was overwhelming. There was conflict on every side. I mean, it was so bad my wife laid in bed the second week we were there and said, "Get me out of here!" She never had said anything like that before.

We stayed five years, but we knew there was something wrong in that congregation. It was non-stop bickering, fighting and conflict. One Sunday I was ready to walk out to preach. My study was behind the sanctuary platform area. There was a hallway leading up to the platform. I walked toward the platform with my mind on the Lord and His word when a little 90 year old lady came up to me shaking her finger in my face complaining about something I did or didn't do that got her upset. It was probably some insignificant thing like the color of my tie, but she was outraged. I walked out on the platform and silently prayed, "Lord, how do I preach to a congregation like this?"

I began to teach my elders about spiritual warfare and how to battle evil through prayer. I told them that spiritual warfare is real and they needed to do something about it. I preached messages on spiritual warfare and the authority of the believer. I taught my elders that when there's conflict in the church and when there's bitterness and anger, there is something going on behind it in the spiritual realm.

In this particular church there was evil. We could feel it. It was strong. It was so strong that there was a fist fight in the foyer of the church between board members! Eventually, I set the elders as spiritual watchmen at the door. I told them, "I want you to stand at the doorway of the church. No one needs to know what you're doing, but I want you to stand against the work of the enemy. I want you to plead the blood of Jesus. I want you to bind the enemy in Jesus' name. You need to pray that no evil will come into this place and that God will stop it.

One Sunday morning a lady was walking into the church and suddenly bent over screaming. "I can't go in. I can't go in. I can't go in, take me home!"

Her family took her home. I heard about it a little while later. I asked who it was. They mentioned her name. It was one of the ladies who was causing great turmoil in the church. When the elders guarded the door against the evil one, she had trouble entering in.

I preached the series on spiritual warfare on Sunday evenings. Our messages were broadcast on the radio every Sunday night. I preached about spiritual warfare and how it affects the church. When I finished the service I went into my study. I noticed the answering machine blinking so I pushed the message button. There came a lady's voice groaning, "I'm dying. I'm dying, I'm dying! Help me, I'm dying!", then hung up. I thought somebody was joking. It sounded like the wicked witch from *The Wizard of Oz* saying, "I'm melting, melting, melting." It gave me goose bumps up and down my neck.

I didn't know who it was immediately. She didn't identify herself. I was all alone, the last person to leave the church. Just then one of my elders happened to come back in because he forgotten his Bible. I asked him to listen to the message. I played it. He said, "Oh, that sends chills up and down my spine."

I asked if he recognized who it was. He answered that he didn't. Then I said, "I think I recognize the voice." It was the voice of this woman that could not enter the church because elders were standing at the church door resisting the enemy. I told him who I thought it sounded like and he agreed. We immediately called her son to ask him to check on her. Sure enough, he found his mother bent over in pain and needing to go to the hospital. As far as I know she was never delivered and remained a thorn in our flesh.

An Evil Spirit in This Place

Luke 10:18-20

The seventy-two returned with joy, saying, "Lord, even the demons are subject to us in your name!" And he said to them, "I saw Satan fall like lightning from heaven. Behold, I have given you authority to tread on serpents and scorpions, and over all the power of the enemy, and nothing shall hurt you. Nevertheless, do not rejoice in this, that the spirits are subject to you, but rejoice that your names are written in heaven."

Sometimes we as rational, logical, humanistic Christians tend to explain things away in natural ways. But often those things that are very strange to us, things that bring oppression, are really attacks from the enemy. We don't always recognize these attacks because we think they come from human beings. We think they come from people with attitudes. Perhaps we think people just don't like us. Instead we ought to see behind the evil. The Apostle Paul said, *"We wrestle not against flesh and blood but against principalities and powers and spiritual wickedness in heavenly places,"* so we ought to understand that we are not wrestling against human factors. Behind every human evil is a demonic spirit that is stirring up trouble. You can find this true all through the Scriptures.

That is not to say that everything that goes bump in the dark, everything that goes wrong, everything that is different or creating difficulties in our lives, is of the devil. But certainly behind the scenes there is an evil one that manipulates people and things. We see that's true in the book of Job. It was natural phenomena that came against Job, but Satan was using those things to discourage him and to get him to turn away from the Lord. There were diseases that afflicted Job, but behind the disease was the destroyer. Behind those scenes God "lifted the curtain" so we could see that it is the evil one who seeks to devour and destroy.

There was a situation in another church that really became very oppressive. It was another church filled with conflict and infighting. Most of the board members told me they hated their church and wanted to leave. There was a nasty split some years before. People were still upset about it. It caused great dissension in the congregation. Even after the people who caused the split left the church, there was left behind the residual effects of unforgiveness, anger and bitterness.

After the first year there we discovered a gross sexual sin that had been behind the scenes for 50 years. It became our responsibility to discipline a man who was involved in homosexual acts within the church and within the community. As you can imagine that did not make us very popular. It was not easy to do go to the whole congregation and expose his sin. Some did not agree with church discipline. Many of them thought we were overdramatizing it. So, in anger they left the church. In one week we lost thirteen families. Of those that remained behind there was certainly an attitude of hatred toward me and toward the elders of the congregation. We could feel it in the church. There was a palpable sense of demonic activity while I preached the word. Worship was stifled. The presence of God was not evident. People were not being saved. People were not getting right with God. . It was as if the word of God was being preached, but the words were falling to the ground and not going into the hearts of the people. I told my elders that there would come a day when we needed to deal with the oppression of the enemy that was prevalent in our church. That time came a couple of months later.

I was in the pulpit having the same kind of problem I'd experienced in other places when there was demonic activity in the church. I was stumbling over words and having difficulty focusing my thoughts. There seemed to be confusion in my own mind how to communicate effectively. As I looked up in the congregation I saw the angry faces of those that hated me. Those faces were hard, hateful, angry and defiant.

I had told the elders that if that would ever happen I would stop my preaching and allow about 10 seconds to go by in silence, then I would say, "Elders I need you now!" I had instructed them to go to the four corners of our sanctuary and stand as men on guard to prayerfully resist, rebuke and bind the enemy in Jesus' name. None of them had ever had experience with this so it was all theoretical up to that point.

When that day came I was impressed by the response of my elders. I stopped my preaching in the middle of a sentence. I was silent for at least 10 seconds. I looked at the congregation. I looked at every face. Then I said, "Elders I need you now!"

Immediately three of my elders got up and went to the three corners of the sanctuary. One elder was missing. Later I discovered he had been monitoring the hallways in the children's wing. There was no amplification of the message on speakers going back to those rooms. He told me later, "Pastor, I kid you not; I heard a voice say, 'The pastor needs you now!'" Then he added, "Pastor I am not a woo-woo person. I am not a Pentecostal. I don't hear voices. I'm not even sure if I believe in that kind of stuff, but this morning I heard an audible voice say, 'Pastor Dick needs you now!' I ran to the sanctuary, took my place in one of the corners and stood there resisting and rebuking the enemy in Jesus' name."

That morning the evil spirit of bitterness broke. That evil spirit of anger broke. That evil spirit of oppression broke. The people who hated me left and never came back to church after that Sunday. God delivered us from the oppression of the enemy.

Angels Surrounded the Church

A few weeks before this I received a letter from a person in the community. In that letter she said, "Pastor you don't know me and I don't know you, but as I was I was praying God revealed to me that there is a great oppression in your church. I don't need to know what that is, but I wanted to tell you that as I was praying I had a vision, in that vision I saw angels surrounding the whole property of the church. Pastor the angels were there in warfare garments with sword in hand opposing the enemy. God has told me to write you and let you know that you are not alone. The battle is not yours, the battle is the Lord's and God will be the victor.

What a wonderful experience to know that God is listening to our prayers. God hears our cries. God knows what needs to be done.

Chapter 13

God's Voice

*And your ears shall hear a word behind you,
saying, "This is the way, walk in it,"
when you turn to the right or
when you turn to the left.
Isaiah 30:21*

God Speaks to His Children

John 10:27
My sheep hear my voice and I know them, and they follow me.

When I tell my stories I often share that God speaks to me. Some people have asked me, "How does God speak to you? Is it an audible voice? Is it an impression? Is it a whisper that you hear in your ears, or in your mind? How is it that God speaks to you and how would I ever know if he speaks to me?"

That is difficult to answer because God speaks to each one of us in different ways. It's like the story of Samuel. When Samuel was really young he heard a voice in his sleep. It was an audible voice saying "Samuel, Samuel!" When Eli, the priest, finally recognized that God was trying to speak to Samuel he told him, "The next time you hear that voice and it calls your name, answer the voice and say, 'Here am I your servant is listening.'"

Sometimes I think that we don't hear the voice of God because we're not listening for it. Many times we don't believe that God speaks today. We have become unbelieving believers, cessationists, who think that all the miracles ceased with the Apostles.

I was sharing my stories with a few pastors I was coaching. When I shared that God had spoken to me and was leading me to do something, one of the young men got very upset. As a matter fact, he literally got in my face, shook his finger at me, and shouted with a loud voice. He was like a madman, furious that I would say that God spoke to me. Then he emphatically told me that God doesn't speak anymore. God's voice stopped with the Apostles. We have the Bible and we need nothing more. There is no way that God speaks to anyone today. He went on to say anyone that says otherwise is lying.

I was taken back by that. Here I was coaching and mentoring young inexperienced pastors and one got so upset he yelled at me. I was so thankful for one of the other young men who took up his responsibility to rebuke that young man. He did so by saying, "No, you are out of order. When you say God does not speak today you are saying God is just like the gods of the pagans. He has no mouth so he cannot speak. He has no eyes, so he cannot see. He has no ears, so he cannot hear, and that is not the gospel of Jesus Christ." Jesus said, *"My sheep hear my voice and they follow me."* He did not say, "My sheep have only the written word of God." Think about it. Who gagged God that He is not allowed to speak anymore? God is God. He speaks today as well as yesterday.

My Mom's Discernment

John 16:13
But when he, the Spirit of truth, comes, he will guide you into all the truth. He will not speak on his own; he will speak only what he hears, and he will tell you what is yet to come.

My mother had a special gift of discernment. She was able to hear from God. She was attuned to His whisper. She had the gift of intercession, that is, she knew what to pray for when there was no clue in the world what she should pray. Here's an example.

My brothers and I knew about that gift in my mother, I was going on a double date with my brother. We were going into Ohio, about two hours from home. We took the girls out to a Youth for Christ rally then stopped at a restaurant in Toledo for dessert. We had a good time.

It was late when we started back home to Monroe, Michigan. I was driving my little red six-cylinder Ford Falcon. I started to pass another car on a dark two-lane road. Suddenly, a truck came toward us out of nowhere.. It was barreling toward us at a high speed and was going to hit us head on. I couldn't pull back into my lane since the car I was passing was blocking me, and I couldn't go to the left into a deep ditch. So, I shifted the car into the second gear to get more power, and slammed on the gas. My brother was white knuckled looking at me and screaming, "We are going to die!" We barely got back into my lane by inches as that truck sped past us. I knew we should have been killed. It would have taken a miracle to get us safely back onto my side of the road. My brother Mike looked at me and said, "Mom's going to know. Mom will know this happened, you watch and see."

We got home late that night but mom wasn't up. When we got up for breakfast the next morning my little brother was sitting at the table eating a bowl of cereal and grinning. I asked what he thought was so funny. He replied, "Oh mom, she's going cuckoo. She went nuts last night. She got everyone up with her panic attacks. She said, "Mike and Dick are in trouble! Pray! Everybody plead the blood of Jesus. Oh, Lord Jesus, protect them. Oh Lord, put the angel of the Lord around them." He said she went on like this for 15 or 20 minutes, praying and pleading the blood of Jesus." Then he said, "You know, that's just mom." I asked what time that had happened. It was the exact time that we were passing the car. Mom knew. God speaks to Mom.

"Go Drive Your Car"

Acts 8:26-27
Now an angel of the Lord said to Philip, "Go south to the road—the desert road—that goes down from Jerusalem to Gaza." So he started out, and on his way he met an Ethiopian.

I was a young pastor in my first church in Clymer, Pennsylvania. I had specific disciplines I used to help me learn how to do ministry. I had always made it my point to ask other pastors what their disciplines were and how they found time for prayer and preparing for messages. Out of those interviews I learned a few things and began to incorporate them into my own life as my spiritual disciplines. One of those disciplines was that from 8 o'clock in the morning until noon every day I was to be in my office praying, studying and preparing my heart for the messages on Sunday morning, Sunday night, Wednesday, and Sunday school and all the other speaking engagements that I had.

Since my study was connected to our house I instructed Marilyn that the children were not to barge into my office during those hours. My door was closed and the phone was turned off, so I would not be disturbed. When I am listening to God I am not to listen to any other voices. I only allow interruptions for emergencies.

One morning I was sitting in my office praying and studying. I was preparing a message for a Wednesday night Bible study. As I was intently looking into the word of God, writing an outline and making notes for myself, I suddenly got an impression that I needed to get in the car and drive. My immediate response was to resist that temptation. I was studying. I was before the Lord. I was in my time of prayer. I was not going to interrupt it with some emotional temptation to go for a drive in my car. A few minutes later the impression came again, but this time it seemed more like an inner voice. My immediate response was to resist the temptation as a distraction from the enemy. .

I said to myself, "No Lord, that's not You. You can't be telling me to get in the car and drive because You told me to be in my study and to give myself to prayer."

The third time the voice came it was very clear that I was to get in the car and drive. At this point I said, "Okay Lord, I don't understand this, but I will obey. Did I not just hear You say get in the car and drive? The voice came again and said, "Yes, get in the car and drive. You know my voice."

I obeyed. I got in the car and started driving not knowing where to go. I remember saying to myself as I drove away, "What am I doing? Why am

I listening to this voice telling me to drive? There's no reason for me to go driving at this time of day."

But the voice kept assuring me I was doing the right thing, so I kept driving. I got to the next town, which was Indiana, a much larger town than our little village of Clymer. I got to the first traffic light and the car stalled. Now I was really frustrated. Here I was in the middle of a morning, when I was supposed to be studying, and I was driving nine miles to the next town and trouble struck. I was mad at myself for listening to that voice. I told myself to never again listen to a voice telling me to do something contrary what God has already instructed me to do.

There were honking horns and cars moving around me. I tried to figure out what to do about the car. It wouldn't start, so I got out of the car and lifted the hood. As I looked at it I realized there was a gas station on the opposite corner. Evidently one of the mechanics saw this happening and came over to help to me. He helped me push the car into the gas station to get it started. He introduced himself, told me his name and I told him mine. He asked where I lived and where I worked. I told him Clymer, Pennsylvania and shared that I was pastor of the Christian and Missionary Alliance Church in Clymer.

He looked up surprised and told me that was his granddad's church. He had grown up in that church. As we continued to converse he shared with me that he had given his life to Christ at some point in a Vacation Bible School a long time before but he was no longer walking with God.

That gave me the opportunity to witness and share Christ with him, I encouraged him to come back to church. I invited him to visit us and allow God to work in his heart. The end of that story is that eventually he did come to church with his family, got right with God and began to live for the Lord.

So once again I had to evaluate: Was God speaking at that moment or was it another voice? My answer to that is that it was clearly God's voice because God leads his dear children along.

The Word of God says, *"And your ears shall hear a word behind you, saying, 'This is the way, walk in it,' when you turn to the right or when you turn to the left."* — Isaiah 30:21

A Woman on the Turnpike

Luke 10:30-34
But a Samaritan, as he traveled, came where the man was; and when he saw him, he took pity on him. He went to him and bandaged his wounds, pouring on oil and wine. Then he put the man on his own donkey, brought him to an inn and took care of him.

It was early in my ministry. I was serving in Clymer, Pennsylvania. We were traveling from Pennsylvania to New Jersey to visit Marilyn's parents. We were using the Pennsylvania Turnpike. The Pennsylvania Turnpike is a very busy toll road and I don't normally stop along a busy road to help stranded cars. There are phone stations every 100 yards or so for such emergencies. It was raining and I could see up ahead of me a car was parked on the side of the road with its trunk open. It obviously had a flat tire. Normally I would pass by and hope that they had called somebody to get help. As I passed by immediately I felt the Lord say I should stop and help the lady. The impression was strong that I needed to stop to help this lady. I did. I had passed her, so I pulled off the highway and backed up to where she was.

I got out of the car and offered my services and she was grateful. I began the process of changing her tire while she held an umbrella over me. As I changed the tire she asked me who I was. I told her who I was and that I was a pastor of a church in Clymer, Pennsylvania. That led to a conversation about her life. She shared with me many of the difficulties that she was facing. One of those difficulties was her marriage. Over a period of a half hour or so she shared with me all the troubles she was going through. I gave her my advice and showed her some Scriptures. She told me her name. I don't think I ever gave her my address, but when we finished I prayed with her and then I left.

I thought no more about that incident for more than 40 years. Then I received a letter in Grove City where we were living at the time. I thought it was a strange address and a name I did not recognize. I didn't know who was writing, but I opened the letter to find it was this woman that I helped on the turnpike some 43 years before. She had remembered me and that I had prayed and counseled her. She said she found my name and address somewhere and thought that she should write to me and let me know what happened. She shared with me how God worked in her heart and life and that the prayer that I offered was an encouragement to her. Eventually God resolved the issues of her marriage and she moved on to walk with the Lord.

Chapter 14

God's Anointings

"The Spirit of the LORD began to move him at times in the camp."
Judges 13:25

Nyack College Day of Prayer

Revelation 3:8
See, I have placed before you an open door that no one can shut. I know that you have little strength, yet you have kept my word and have not denied my name.

Throughout my ministry God has given me great opportunities and open doors that were unexpected. While I was serving as a pastor in Pitman, New Jersey I received an invitation from Nyack College, my alma mater, to be the keynote speaker to the men on their Day of Prayer. It was an awesome responsibility and privilege. I was excited about it but I was also nervous. I was going back to the college where I spent six years and would be preaching to the male student body. There was a well known popular women's lecturer and author who was speaking to the women on that Day of Prayer.

I think it helped that I was acquainted with the dean of students who was in charge of scheduling speakers for that day. He knew of me and I had received high recommendations that I would be a good speaker for the Day of Prayer.

We gathered together in the chapel for the service. The men filled the seats. It was crowded. People were everywhere, even up in the balcony. There were professors who had taught me when I was in college, men from Alliance Theological Seminary, along with missionaries and pastors.

The service began with a wonderful time of worship. When the time came for me to speak the dean introduced me and turned the platform over to me. I chose to speak on spiritual warfare using Ephesians 6:12 as the text. I told some stories about spiritual warfare and demonic activity and about the difficulties we faced in Brazil. I also shared some personal struggles with demonic oppression. I don't remember exactly what I said but while I was speaking I sensed the Lord anointing my heart and lips to speak clearly. I could see that men were wrapped up in what I was saying and they seemed to be very responsive.

Of course, I was conscious it wasn't my service. I was just speaker for the hour. The instructions were that when I was finished preaching I would sit down and they would close the service. When I came to the end of my message I finished, turned to the dean of students and asked it he would come to close the service, He paused and stood at the podium for a moment then turned around to me and said, "Dick, I think you need to close the service. You need to give an invitation." Not knowing what else to do, I stood up and just looked at the men and said, "If any of you need to get some things right with God, or if you need to seek the Lord for His deliverance, the altar is open. I will be glad to pray with you."

That's all I said and I sat down. They played a closing song but even before the song began men started to move to the altar. Some students ran to the altar. The altar was filled. They were double lined around the front of the sanctuary. They were in the front pews. They were praying together in small groups of students around the room.

They lined up as I began to pray for students. I would ask them what I should pray for, then lay hands on them and pray. I prayed for one person after another. I was unaware of time passing but finally the dean of students interrupted my prayer time. He grabbed my arm and said, "Dick you're going to overwhelm yourself. You need to stop. You need to go take a break and get lunch. You've been here two hours praying with students."

I was amazed. I didn't sense that two hours had gone by. It was a wonderful and thrilling moment in my life and ministry to have a part in what God was doing in the lives of these young people.

It was many years later while I was serving in Pennsylvania that one of those students happened to be there visiting. He actually grew up in Grove City and he was now a missionary for the Christian Missionary Alliance in Russia. He came to visit his parents and his old home church. I introduced myself and he said. "I know who you are. I was at Nyack when you preached the Day of Prayer. I can tell you exactly what you preached and give your entire outline. He remembered the movement of the Spirit in that place and he said he was so impacted that day that he knew God's hand was on my life.

The College of Prayer

Judges 13:25
And *the Spirit* of Jehovah *began to move* him (Samson). ...
And *the Spirit* of the Lord *began to go* out with him in the camp of Dan.

Perhaps one of the most unusual situations in which God spoke occurred when I was at the College of Prayer retreat in Beulah Beach, Ohio. About 25 people were there gathered together to learn more about prayer and to spend time alone with God. The speaker had lectured for hours on end and I was getting a little bit antsy wanting to spend some time alone with the Lord. So, I spoke to one of the leaders that I did not want to offend him but I would not be at the next sessions because I was spending some time in fasting and prayer and I would join them later.

He allowed me to do that. I spent the entire day fasting and praying and seeking the Lord. One of the things that the Lord was instructing me on was how to spend time alone with him and be quiet, to be still. I was not a still person. I always found it difficult to do, so this was a time of the Lord teaching me one of the disciplines of prayer.

Throughout that day I spent time walking in the woods and over the campus praying and worshiping. I did a lot of walking and talking with God. I spent most of the day outdoors, and sometimes in my room on my face before the Lord, praying and seeking the Lord, opening the Scriptures, and asking God for a word from Him.

When evening came I got back to my room. The others had already had their supper and I was back in my room looking forward to spending two or three hours in the evening spending time alone with God, writing in my journal, reading the Bible, and doing those kinds of things that quiet my heart.

It was seven o'clock in the evening and I knew the group was going to have a communion service. I told the Lord I was going to skip the communion service in favor of spending more time alone with Him. At that point the Lord impressed on me, "I want you to go to the communion service." I responded, "No, Lord, I'm not going to the communion service. That will just disrupt my whole flow of quietness. I've spent a whole day with You and I'm longing for more. I don't want to get out there and start talking to people. I don't want a lot of noise. I just want to be quiet." Again, the Lord said, "I want you to get up and go to the communion service." I resisted.

The third time the Lord spoke it became very clear that God was not going to leave me alone on this matter. He wanted me to go to the communion service. Finally the Lord won out and I consented to go. They were meeting in the lower level of the building. I entered by the back way and took the last seat at the back of the crowd. I sat down and listened to the person who was speaking. A few minutes after I arrived the man leading stopped in the middle of his talk. He turned toward me and said, "The Lord has a word for us from Dick LaFountain." That shocked me. That man had only just met me; he didn't know me well enough to call on me to speak.

I'm sure he must have heard from the Lord, but I certainly didn't know I had a word from the Lord. My mind was not on the communion service. My mind was not on ministering to other people. My mind was not on encouraging others. I was there because the Lord told me to be there. But the leader felt strongly that the Lord had a word for them through me, so I had to share my heart.

One of the things I had observed in that entire day of prayer and fasting was the delight that I had in the Lord. The joy of the Lord I had once lost had returned. I was on cloud nine. I was delighting in the Lord. Throughout the day as I was walking in intimate fellowship with the Lord the song *In the Garden* kept running through my mind.

> "I come to the garden alone, while the dew is still on the roses, and the voice I hear falling on my ear the Son of God discloses, And He walks with me, and He talks with me, and He tells me I am His own, and the joy we share as we tarry there, none other has ever known.

Immediately the Lord told me to share with them my story of lost joy and how the Lord had restored my soul. Reluctantly I stood up and shared that I had just spent the entire day with the Lord in quiet communion. I shared the joy the Lord brought to me in my day of fasting and prayer. I went on to tell them a little of the story of Aimee's death in Brazil and how I had lost my joy. I had lost my faith and was in a miserable state. I told them how over a period of years the Lord had restored the joy of my salvation through intimate prayer.

At that point I would have just sat down and they would've gone on with the communion service. But again, the Lord prompted me to say, "I want you to experience that joy of the Lord. I want to pray over those who have lost the joy of their salvation. I asked, "How many of you have lost the joy of your salvation and how many long to enjoy the presence of the Lord?" All around the room hands were raised. Of the 25 people there must have been 20 who raised their hands indicating that they wanted prayer to restore the joy of the Lord in their lives.

I did not want to do this alone so I called on several of the leaders to join me in prayer. We gathered around each one to lay hands on them and pray for them.

This is where a very unusual thing happened. As I laid my hands on the first person to pray I saw a dark well and as I prayed things came up out of the well, things that I could identify, things that I should pray for.

I know my brother David had this gift of discernment and revelation. Often when he prays for people God reveals things that he should pray for. He would find out later that those were the exactly the things that

God had spoken to those people about. I thought, "Wow, this is really an unusual experience."

I went to the next person to pray, and as I prayed for them the same thing happened. I saw this deep well out of which came things for me to pray about. I prayed for those things then I moved onto the next person.

I was astounded. I was praying for these people and telling them what was going on in their lives without ever knowing anything about them. I was starting to feel like a fool. I didn't know if anything I was saying made any sense to them. Even as I was praying I was thinking, "Lord, am I making this up? If I'm doing something foolish stop me. I tried to resist the Holy Spirit and not say anything about their lives, yet the same thing happened with each person.

For each person that I prayed for there was a visible well and out of that well things came forward that I needed to pray for. I tried to avoid mentioning those things by name, but the words just came to me as the Holy Spirit gave me utterance. I continued down the line to the last person. I was actually fearful, wondering whether I was doing something by God's leading, or whether I was just hungry spending a day in fasting. Was I imagining things?

I came to the last woman. As I laid hands on her to pray suddenly there was a dark well and out of that well came some very evil things for me to pray for. I can't tell you exactly what I saw, but I saw some very specific things about this woman's marriage. It was in trouble and she was struggling with a great temptation and God wanted to deliver her from that temptation. As I saw those things I whispered to the Lord in my mind, "Lord, I can't say those things out loud, that would be embarrassing for her." So the Lord said, "Pray around it." So I prayed around it the best I could without referring directly to what I was seeing...

When I finished praying for her they served communion. When they finished communion I made a beeline out of that room. I didn't stay to talk to anyone. I didn't stay to confirm with anyone about whether what I prayed for was correct or incorrect. I was embarrassed. I ran back to my room, fell on my face before the Lord and wept. I said, "Oh Lord, oh Lord, what have I done? Have I just made a fool of myself? Have I just made a fool of prayer? What was I doing? What was I thinking? What was I saying? Why did I pray like that?"

I continued to pray in my room perhaps for an hour and a half and then I went to bed still feeling this angst that I did something foolish. What I did was not normal. It was weird. I was acting like a charismatic Pentecostal.

The next morning I got up for breakfast. I was hungry since I had eaten nothing the day before. As I was on my way to the cafeteria a young man approached me who I had prayed for the night before. I thought, "Oh no, here it comes. Now I'm going to catch it." But the young man approached me and said, "Dick how did you know how to pray for me last night? You prayed exactly what was going on in my life? No one knew what was going in my life. No one could have known. How did you know what to pray for?"

I answered him and called him by name, "John, I don't know what I prayed for last night. I don't remember what I prayed for you. In fact, I don't remember what I prayed for anyone last night. I prayed as the Spirit gave me the words. I prayed as the Lord revealed things to me." He responded by saying that during the College of Prayer one of the lecturers had taught about "prophetic praying" and what I did was prophetic praying. Then he thanked me for listening to the Holy Spirit.

As I entered into the cafeteria I took my tray and went through the line and got my food. I chose to sit alone by myself as I often do. As I sat down and began to eat my breakfast other people approached me and said something very similar, that what I had prayed for was right on.

I deliberately avoided the young lady I had prayed for. I didn't want to have to deal with her face-to-face. I continued to pray over what to do about those prayers that I offered, and what to do about this particular young lady. I said, "Lord, what am I supposed to do with that information? Am I supposed to tell someone? Am I supposed to confront her?" The Lord answered, "No, what I want you to do is to continue to pray for her. That's why I revealed those things to you, so that you could pray."

For an entire year I prayed for that young lady by name. I remembered who she was. I knew her face very well and I prayed desperately that the Lord would deliver her from her temptation or whatever it was that she was facing.

A year later I went back for another conference at the College of Prayer at Beulah Beach. I was certain that I would probably run into this young lady, but I wanted to avoid her. I arrived at lunchtime. I went to the cafeteria, picked up my tray, went through the line, served myself, and again sat alone as I am accustomed to do.

As I bowed my head to pray over the food and for the Lord to guide us in our studies, this young lady walked into the cafeteria. She went through the line, and got her food. Then she looked around the room and made a beeline straight for me. I thought, "Oh no. Here she comes." She came up and sat down right across from me and looked at me and said, "Dick, you probably don't remember me, but you prayed for me last year. Do you remember that?" (Of course, I remembered!) I told her, "Yes, I remember very clearly praying for you last year." Then she told me her story.

She told me that when I approached her to pray for her God pointed to the sins that were in her life. She said one particular sin was above all of them. She had fallen in love with an elder in her church, nothing sexual had happened, but they had passed notes back-and-forth and communicated with each other by email. She was ready to leave her husband and run off with this elder. She said, "When you prayed for me the Spirit of God gave me a deep conviction of my sin and as you prayed for me you laid your finger exactly on it. I felt like you knew my exact sin. You could see my heart. You were pointing at it. You were rebuking the enemy, and you were standing in the gap on my behalf."

Then she added that when she went home she broke off that relationship with the elder. She confessed her sins and her temptation to her husband and got marriage counseling. She shared they were restored as a couple and then God gave her a prayer ministry for other people in the church. She became a prayer leader for their zone within the district. She concluded, "I just wanted to thank you for listening to the Holy Spirit and allowing the Lord to pray through you. Thank you."

God Wants to Heal the Deaf

Mark 10:51
*"What do you want me to do for you?" Jesus asked him.
The blind man said, "Rabbi, I want to see."*

The next significant story about God speaking to my heart took place in to a town called Charleroi in western Pennsylvania. I was doing our conference speaking on prayer. Every weekend I was in a different church speaking on prayer and encouraging people to believe God for great things. I had been doing this for a number of years. In Charleroi I had met with the pastor, who was an acquaintance of mine. We talked about the conference. He told me about the church and what had taken place many years before over the charismatic movement that split the church. He cautioned me not to do anything charismatic in these meetings. I assured him that I was not a Pentecostal or charismatic, at least not in my perception.

The service began with wonderful worship. The songs were anointed and moving. There was one particular song that was sung and it was the song just before the message. The words went like this:

> *"Lord, hear our cry. Come heal our land*
> *Breath life into these dry and thirsty souls*
> *Lord, hear our prayer. Forgive our sin*
> *And as we call on Your name*
> *Would You make this a place*
> *For Your glory to dwell*
>
> <u>*Chorus*</u>*:*
> *Open the blind eyes. Unlock the deaf ears*
> *Come to Your people As we draw near*
> *Hear us from heaven. Touch our generation*
> *We are Your people Crying out in desperation*

As they were singing they repeated that verse over and over again. I was worshipping, preparing my heart for the message of the morning. My message was not about healing. My message was about prayer. But while I was worshiping the voice of the Lord came very clearly to my mind. He said. "I want you to tell people I want to heal them." I responded, "Lord, that's not permitted here. The pastor has asked me not to do that."

A second time the Lord spoke and said, "No, I want you to invite people to be healed and specifically I want you to invite them to be healed of their hearing loss. I want to unlock deaf ears." I argued with the Lord, "Lord I can't do that. The pastor has asked me not to do anything charismatic and I need to obey him."

The third time the Lord spoke it was very clear that God was speaking to my heart. Just before I stepped up for the message the Lord spoke again, "You know my voice and I am instructing you. I want you to stand up and tell people I want to heal those who are deaf and those who have hearing loss."

By the time I stood in the pulpit I was still wrestling with God, but my heart was burning. I knew what I needed to do. First, I apologized for what I was about to do. I explained that I had never done this before, but I was being urged to do so by the Holy Spirit. Then I told them that the Lord had spoken to me and He had repeated it at least three times, "I want to heal those here this morning that have hearing difficulties."

As I started to speak the words just flowed out of me. I described the hearing loss, the ringing in the ears, the dizziness and other symptoms the Lord was indicating He wanted to heal. I said, "Without further ado, I'm going to pray for the hearing impaired this morning that the Lord would open your ears." I did so briefly and moved on with the service.

I thought no more about that until after the service was over. People came to the altar. People were being prayed for and being revived and were rededicating their lives to the Lord.

No sooner was the service over than an elderly man came running over to me and said, "Pastor Dick, Pastor Dick! I have to tell you what the Lord has done." Then he proceeded to tell me that he had arrived at the service with his wife and realized that his hearing aid was not working. He hadn't replaced the batteries. He said it was very frustrating because in the early part of the service he couldn't hear what was going on. He couldn't understand the music. He couldn't understand what people were saying. He reported that he was really distraught that he wouldn't be able to hear what my message was. When I stood up and said, "The Lord said I want to heal those that have hearing difficulties today." He exclaimed, "I knew that the Lord was speaking to me and the Lord wanted to heal my ears!" When you prayed I raised my hand and received the healing that I needed. Immediately my hearing aid didn't start working, but my ears started working. I took my hearing aid out and I could hear clearly the entire service. Thank you for obeying the Lord.

Another man came forward after most of the people had left. He also identified with being a man of hearing loss. He said, "What you said on the platform was exactly what I said to my wife on the way to church. You described word for word what I told my wife about my hearing." Evidently I had said something about the ringing in the ears and the deafness that comes and goes and described him exactly. "So when you said that, I knew that God was speaking to my heart. I knew that God wanted to heal my hearing."

"But," he confessed, "I was not healed this morning because I have lost my faith. I can't believe God for healing anymore." He explained to me that he had lost his faith in the Lord. He had a grandson who had cancer and they had prayed for years and asked God to heal him. They went to healing conferences and trusted the Lord to heal his young body. But God did not heal him and that young child died. He explained that when his grandson died his faith in God's healing power also died.

He went on to tell me that he didn't come forward because he couldn't believe the Lord anymore. He was weeping as he told me this. I told him, "Let's pray anyway. A man came to Jesus with his sick son and begged Jesus saying, 'Lord I believe. Help my unbelief.' Let me pray that the Lord helps your unbelief and restores to you the joy of your salvation and restores to you the faith in what God can do. I prayed for the man. I took his name down so I could continue to pray for him. The service ended, we had a light lunch, followed by an afternoon conference with another 2 to 2 1/2 hours of lectures.

I was fearful of what was going to happen with the pastor after this, even though we saw great movement of the Spirit of God in that church service and obviously the anointing of the Lord was upon everything that was done. I was afraid the pastor was going to come back to me and scold me, or at least report me to the District Superintendent as not being submissive to the authority that was given to him, but he did not.

It was months later I got a letter from the pastor. When I saw the letter I was concerned about what I was going to read. I opened the letter. He reviewed what we had talked about prior to the conference and his expectation that I should not do any "woo woo" stuff or charismatic things in the service. He acknowledged that I disobeyed and had gone ahead and done so anyway. Then he said it was okay, what I had done was in order and certainly proper and appropriate. He had heard about one man that was healed and another man that was hoping to trust the Lord for his healing.

But the reason he was writing was because there was another man in that service that he knew nothing about. He was an executive in a large corporation. He had recently started coming to their church and had been trusting the Lord for a miracle in his life. Unknown to the pastor, this man had a hearing problem. He had been overlooked for promotions in his business because of his hearing loss. He had his hearing tested and they found it was greatly diminished and because of that they would not give him a promotion. He said he was in the service that day when Pastor Dick described the hearing loss. He said that was him. He told his pastor, "I knew immediately the Lord was speaking to my heart that God wanted to heal my hearing. So, I too raised my hand as he prayed and asked the Lord to heal my ears and bring back my hearing.

He said it didn't happen instantaneously that day, but over a period of the next months his hearing was completely restored. He went back for testing and they found his hearing was perfect. Best of all, he got the promotion that was promised to him.

The pastor said, "This man came to me to tell me his testimony and in doing so he asked me to communicate with you to let you know that you were led by the Spirit of God that day. You did nothing inappropriate at all and he wanted to thank you for listening to the voice of the Holy Spirit.

God Wants to Heal the Lame

Acts 3:6
*Peter said, "I have no silver or gold,
but what I have I give you; in the name of
Jesus Christ of Nazareth, stand up and walk."*

This incident took place at a *Rekindle the Flame* prayer conference. I had been asked to be a co-leader in the conference. It was held in our western Pennsylvania District. We gathered together the night before the conference and had a time of prayer and seeking the Lord's presence and blessing. There were probably nine or ten people gathered together. While I prayed I saw a vision. I've never had a vision like this before. I was down on my knees in one of the front pews praying and asking God to do his work among us and asking him what he wanted me to do.

I had a very clear picture of a man in a wheelchair with bands on his legs. He was crippled. He was coming into the *Rekindle the Flame* conference. I saw him coming through the doors. I saw him wheeling himself down the hallway. As I looked I was astounded because I recognized who he was. Many years before while we were preparing to go to Brazil it was required that we get an attorney to draw up a will for us. We had used a particular lawyer that was significant in the Christian and Missionary Alliance. I had not seen him for many years. It was very unusual that I would see him in Western Pennsylvania. I knew that he did not live in Western Pennsylvania. As far as I knew he still lived in New York. When I saw this very clear vision I asked the Lord, "What is this? Why are you revealing this to me?" The Lord spoke very clearly to my heart and said "I want to heal him."

After we dismissed the meeting I met with some of the leaders and told them about the vision I saw in prayer. They said it certainly sounded like a vision from the Lord but the test would really be if this man happened to show up here, or somebody similar to him, then you will know that it is from the Lord. I went home that evening and told Marilyn about the vision. I was very concerned about seeing visions and maybe having prophetic words that were not from the Lord but from my own heart.

The next day I went to the conference. I was there early to help get things set up. As we were setting up chairs I happened to be crossing the entrance way of the church. I looked up and to my shock I saw the same man I had seen in my vision wheeling himself into the church. When I got closer I looked at him and recognized it was the lawyer! I got goose bumps up and down my spine. I met him at the door and called him by name and said, "What are you doing here?" He said, "Well, I heard about the *Rekindle the Flame* conference and I came to hear what was going to be said. I said, "Excuse me for being shocked to see you but I thought you lived in New York, and people in New York don't usually travel to Western Pennsylvania for a conference." He replied that he was retired and lived in Florida now but when he heard about the conference he sensed the Lord prompting him to go. So, he came.

I quickly gathered together the leaders that prayed with me the night before and I told them, "He's here! He's here! The man I saw in my vision last night is really here." Then I asked them what they thought I should do. Should I call him out in the conference and tell him of my vision and what the Lord said? They all thought it was best later in the conference before a healing service to tell of my vision in general terms, not mentioning specifically the wheel chair or his polio and see if he responds.

That sounded reasonable, so I agreed. Although I felt in my heart that was not what God wanted us to do, that God wanted me to say specifically, "Brother, I had a vision of you yesterday and God said, 'I want to heal you, if you can trust me.'"

After the lectures of the day were finished, we had a time of prayer for healing. The leader called on me to share my vision from the Lord. I came forward and shared the vision I had seen and what the Lord wanted to do. I did not describe him in a wheelchair, instead I described someone that had problem walking, and that it's been there for many years and they desperately needed the Lord to heal them. I said, "This evening the Lord is calling on you, if you have the faith to believe Him, he said He wants to heal you tonight."

With that we gave the invitation. Many people came forward and were prayed for. Some were healed, some were not. Three men gave testimonies that night that they felt they were the person in that vision and that God had spoken to them that they needed to trust God for their serious back injuries. The three of them were healed.

But the lawyer did not come forward. It broke my heart. I wasn't sure what to do about that. About the time we were cleaning up and ready to close the doors I saw he was still in the room. He slowly wheeled himself up to me and pulled me aside and said, "Dick I need to talk to you. I have no doubt that I was the one that you saw in that vision. I knew that as soon as I came in and you said "What are you doing here!" that something unusual was happening. I knew that the Lord was offering me another opportunity to trust him to heal my body."

Then he told me his story. In tears he told me about his polio as a young child and the years that he spent seeking the Lord for healing. He had gone to many healing conferences. He had been to Oral Roberts. He'd gone to every possible charismatic meeting that would offer healing. But the Lord never healed him. So he took the passage of 2 Corinthians where the apostle Paul said, *"My grace is sufficient for you my strength is made perfect in your weakness."* He said he went away to college then on to law school and got his degree and became an attorney. He worked for the Christian Missionary Alliance as part of his missionary service to the Lord. Then he concluded, "Dick, many years ago I gave up asking the Lord to heal me. Tonight when you shared your vision, my heart was overwhelmed and I began to weep saying, 'Oh God not again. Here we go again, another disappointment!' Dick, I did not have the courage to come forward to be prayed for because you said, 'The Lord said I want to heal you if you have the faith to believe me and trust me.' I do not have the faith to believe God for my healing."

This brother and I wept together. I sobbed as I prayed with him. I told him I was sorry that I had a vision and had to share that with him, but I was to be obedient to the Lord. I had to. He said he understood.

I felt that what had happened was a camaraderie developed between him and me. He asked to have lunch with me the next day and we had a great time together hearing more of his story and more of what God was doing in his life. I had hoped that at that time he would trust the Lord for his healing and ask for the elders to come and anoint him once again. But he did not.

Dan continues to move about in his wheelchair, continues to be the invalid that he has been for so many years. I had to ask myself after all this, "Lord, what were you doing? Why were you bringing that vision if you weren't going to heal him?" Perhaps in heaven we will know.

Chapter 15

God's Restorations

He restoreth my soul.
Psalm 23:5

I will restore to you the years the locust has eaten…You shall eat plenty and be satisfied, and praise the name of the Lord your God, who has dealt wonderously with you.
Joel 2:25

Restored Lost Joy and Faith

1 Peter 5:10
And after you have suffered a little while, the God of all grace, who has called you to his eternal glory in Christ, will himself restore, confirm, strengthen, and establish you.

I want to tell you about the most impactful event of our lives that became the cornerstone of who we are.

We were in Brazil as missionaries. We were serving the Lord faithfully and loving what God was doing, seeing Him do great things. Our 12 year old daughter Aimee went with her girlfriends to cross the road to buy bread at a local store. In the process she was hit by a car, thrown through the air, and suffered massive brain injuries. I happened to be out of the country at the time. I was on route to Argentina. When I arrived in Argentina they gave me the news, desperate news. "Your daughter has been in an accident and she is not expected to live." I cannot possibly tell you the immense pain that brought to my heart.

Being a thousand miles away when your little one is in the moment of life and death is a living torment. It is like hanging between earth and heaven. Marilyn called me on the phone and she said, "Dick, you've got to get back here." I was paralyzed, I couldn't get back. There were no flights until the next day. There was no way to get back. That night was a sleepless night of prevailing prayer. I knelt before God unable to sleep calling on the name of the Lord. I used every principle in every Scripture, and every bit of faith I could muster to hang onto God for a miracle.

The next day I was able to catch the first flight out and got back to Brazil. I was met there by Steve Renicks, my colleague in ministry. We immediately went to the hospital and there I heard the diagnosis that Aimee was brain dead. The doctor told us that though her brain was dead her heart could keep beating for days or even weeks. He explained that soon we would have to decide to unplug the machines and let her body die. We went back home and struggled through that issue of turning off Aimee's life support system.

That night when all of us gathered in our room we prayed and put our hands on Andrew and little Angelica, and said, "Lord, we don't know what you want to do. We want you to heal Aimee, but if not, we don't want to be the ones to pull the plug. We ask you to stop her little heart and take her home, if that is your will."

That was about 11 o'clock at night. At one o'clock in the morning we got a call from the hospital saying Aimee's heart suddenly stopped beating. Aimee was in heaven that day.

I don't tell you that story because I like to tell it. I don't like to tell it at all. I'd like to erase it from my life, but it's there. It's a reality that all of us have to face that sometimes God says "no" to our prayer requests. Sometimes God says "no" when we cry out to him with everything that is in us. We begged and we pleaded and we got mighty men and women of prayer praying for us but God said, "No, I'm not going to answer that one, not the way you wanted."

I've written a book called *Restoring Shattered Faith* because my faith was shattered. My faith was shipwrecked one day in 1982 when our twelve year old daughter died in an accident while we were serving as missionaries in Brazil. It didn't shatter all at once. Adrenaline gets you through for a time. It shattered over a period of time. Looking back on those events of our daughter dying I began to wonder, where was God? Why didn't He answer? Why didn't He save our daughter? Why didn't He heal her? Why didn't He raise her from the dead? We hung onto our faith for two years after her death and continued to serve in Brazil.

Then my world fell apart. My health broke. I had chest pains and an ever increasing band squeezing my brain. At first the doctor thought I had a heart attack. After tests, he said there was nothing wrong with my physical heart. What was wrong was my broken heart that no one could fix. Marilyn and I knew I needed to get out from under the stress of Brazil and get some help. We stood in the kitchen talking about my feelings and Marilyn suggested it was time to go home. I said, "God called me to Brazil and I am not leaving unless they drag me out on a stretcher." That was almost the case. By the time we left I had collapsed from stress. I was on heavy antidepressant medications. I was so sick I hardly remember those last weeks in Brazil. I felt like I was living in a fog.

When we arrived home we met with the officials of our mission and they suggested, and then mandated, that I seek psychological counseling. I didn't want counseling. It was like hearing a diagnosis that I was crazy on top of everything else that happened.

This was two years after Aimee's death. My faith was gone. Life seemed unfair, hopeless, out-of-control. I was angry at God, but didn't know it. It began as disappointment with God, and then it grew to disillusionment with God and His promises. Life felt unreal. The world around me seemed an illusion. I continued to be on heavy medications unable to stay awake for more than a few hours at a time.

I started to see a counselor recommended by our mission. He was a former missionary and understood the stresses of missionary life and tragedies. He was located almost two hours drive from where we were living with Marilyn's parents. The drive was long and I was not well. The sessions were painful. I didn't like the counselor. I didn't want to be there. I hated having to go to a counselor.

Early on in our sessions Dr. Draper told me that he believed I would not stay in counseling. He knew I hated it and would find any excuse to get out of it. He said, "Dick, you will sabotage these sessions so you can stop coming and say it didn't work." I was insulted by that, but it was true. I was looking for a way out of counseling. It was expensive, too far away, and I didn't like the counselor.

I went home that day and told Marilyn what he said. We thought and prayed about it and knew that I really did need to talk to someone about my inner conflicts. We looked at our meager savings accrued during five years overseas and decided we would invest all of that to get this counseling. I took that $1500 to Dr Draper and laid it on the table and asked, "How much counseling will this buy? I'm paying it all up front so I can't quit." He said, "It's enough, and I'll give you a discounted rate so that you are covered for a full year."

We started meeting three times per week, an hour each session. After a month we went to twice a week. Eventually, it would be once a week. I stayed with him for two years of counseling.

During those first months I still was not feeling well. I slept much of the time. One day I received a call from a church that had sponsored us as missionaries. We knew them fairly well. We had visited them before going to Brazil and on our furlough in 1982. They had sponsored our children as their "missionary kids." A friend of mine from college had been the pastor of that church. The head elder called to tell me that my friend Dave had left the church and they were looking for another pastor. He asked if I would consider being their pastor. I told him I didn't feel up to being anyone's pastor and didn't even know if I wanted to preach again. I told him he didn't know what I was going through and that I was unworthy to be a pastor.

How he responded made me cry. He said, "Pastor Dick, we know what you are going through and we want to minister to you as you minister to us." I made a few other excuses and told him he would have to go through the District Superintendent and the whole candidating process. He acknowledged that process but said he wanted me to know they already knew they wanted me to be their pastor.

I didn't want to go to Pitman to be their pastor but I consented to candidate. I was pretty well set on not going there. I did what I always do; I made a list of all the things the Lord would have to do in order to convince me I should go there. When the District Superintendent called to extend a unanimous call I checked my impossible list. God had answered every item on the list, except one. I wanted a fireplace. They did not have one, but we agreed to go there anyway.

Although I became the pastor of the Pitman Alliance Church I was still in bad shape emotionally and spiritually. God had broken his promises to me. I felt God's promises were not true any longer. He took our 12-year-old daughter in a horrible accident, though we cried to him, and perhaps thousands of people across Brazil and America prayed and interceded on our behalf, and God didn't answer. That was devastating.

Shortly after starting with the counselor I made a trip out to Michigan to my hometown. I remember being at the bottom of my well. I felt like I was a low as I could go. I couldn't lift myself out of that pit of despondency. I couldn't see my way clear for anything. It felt like all of God's promises were lies.

I remember driving into a McDonald's (I really had to be depressed to do that) to get my lunch and then parked beside the dumpster. I didn't want to see people. I didn't want to be out in the open. My heart was breaking. I sat in my car weeping bitterly and said, "Lord, I'm giving up on you. I'm giving up on everything that I believed and held dear because it's just not true anymore." My heart said, "Drive west young man. Drive west. Just get in the car and drive and don't stop. Leave your family. Leave everything behind and forget what's happened. Forget about God and start a new life." My heart was fully tempted to do that and it scared me.

In those moments as I sat there next to the dumpster I said, "Lord, I can't believe you anymore. Your promises are not true. It seems like everything I built my life on is bogus. It's wrong. It's incorrect. It's not true at all." In those moments, God spoke to my heart with that still small voice of the Holy Spirit. He challenged me in that moment of my deepest crisis.

He said, "Dick, can you believe me for one thing?" I angrily responded, "Lord, I can't believe you for anything. You've failed me. You haven't heard my cry. You've torn my heart apart. You've torn my life apart. You have torn my ministry apart."

God whispered again, "Can you believe me for just one thing?" Again I sobbed, "I don't know if I can do that. I don't have any faith! Don't ask me to believe!"

Then in frustration I shouted, "What one thing?"
God whispered this to me, "I DO NOT LIE!"

My heart broke. I sobbed and just poured out all of my tears. I said through my tears, "Lord, I wish I could believe that. My faith is gone. I'm empty. I have nothing else." Then God said, "I ask you to believe me for one thing, just this one small thought—I DO NOT LIE. Forget all the other promises. They're all built on this one thing. I do not lie."

In those scary moments I felt like I stood between life and death. With the weakness of my faith at that moment, I said, "Lord, I don't have faith, but if you'll help me, if you give me faith to believe you for that one thought then I'll give you one more chance. I will hang on to that thought."

In that moment God reached down in pity and touched my heart. He gave me faith like a tiny mustard seed. He gave me the minutest little faith to believe one thing. That began a turning point in my recovery. I did an about face. I turned around and drove back to my family, and went into the counseling, and the counseling was built on that one thought. God says, "I do not lie."

During those years of prolonged grief, a broken heart, and broken spirit, God began to restore my soul. Healing does not always come through some immediate miraculous touch as we see so often in the New Testament. This time my healing came over a long period of time. We spent eight years in the Pitman church. It was a place of peace and healing. They indeed ministered to us as we ministered to them.

I began to preach through the book of Romans, which became another way in which the Lord slowly mended my broken heart and restored my faith. Truly the Lord fulfilled his word that *"faith comes by hearing and hearing by the word of God."*

On one occasion I had been disqualifying all the positive input my counselor suggested. He could not get nowhere with my stubborn heart. Finally one day he said, "Dick, if you could stand before God right now and say anything to God, knowing he would not scold you or judge you, what would you say?"

My answer surprised me. I didn't even have to think about it. It was a breakthrough moment. I suddenly blurted out, "I would say, 'God I am angry with you. You are unfair. You are cruel to me. You took away my daughter in a terrible accident. We asked you to spare her life, but you didn't. You let her die. You did not answer prayer. I feel like you are punishing me, and I didn't do anything wrong. I've served you faithfully. I've searched my heart. I did nothing worthy of this punishment. Your promises are not true. You failed me! You lied and I can't trust you anymore!'"

My counselor listened as I cried tears, sobbing as I poured out my anger to God. When I finished ranting he sighed, "Dick, now I think we can get somewhere. Let's start with your anger and accusations against God. I perceive in all that you have told me that you have never really believed God loves you unconditionally. Everything in your spiritual life is about your obedience and God's reward. Nothing is about grace. It's all about your work. You believe your work equals your worth."

He was gentle and wise as he guided me and challenged me to search the Scriptures to find the unconditional love of God, which I never really understood, nor could I see it. I went through the Scriptures asking God to show me if unconditional love was really true. That led me to Romans and justification by faith and salvation by grace alone. I knew all that in my head, but I did not know it in my heart.

Through the word of God, God healed my broken theology and my wounded heart. He restored to me the joy of my salvation.

Renewed, Refreshed and Restored

Psalm 81:5-7
I heard an unknown voice say: "I removed the burden from their shoulders; their hands were set free from the pots. In your distress you called and I rescued you, I answered you out of a thundercloud;"

Some years later I was doing research on unreached people groups. I was compiling the information and sharing it with a friend that lived across the country. Together we had written and compiled over 2000 profiles of people who have never heard the Gospel. This was my burden and my concern. This was my way of continuing my missions calling while serving in the States.

A few years before this I had started an unofficial website for the Christian and Missionary Alliance. They recognized its value and gave me permission to continue doing it.

One of the things I did with my own website was to do teach online. I had online Bible studies on the *Life of Christ* which were conducted like a real classroom situation. We had quizzes and tests and I asked people to write papers and dialogue with each other over the subject matter. I did the basic lectures in print format then the students would gather together online through *instant messenger* to discuss the material we were studying. It was quite an extensive program of teaching and training people about the *Life of Christ*. I did this for several years having anywhere from 10 to 20 students in each semester. It was enjoyable to be doing something outside of pastoral ministry.

As I developed the unofficial website for the Christian and Missionary Alliance I had opportunities to visit the Alliance headquarters in Colorado Springs to get more information about unreached people groups. On one particular visit I carried the 10 discs of unreached people with me. A friend of mine who worked at the national office knew some of the leaders of other missions organizations focused on unreached people groups. Together we went to visit them. I told them that we had 2000 profiles of unreached people groups. They were astounded and said that was amazing and admitted they did not have access to any resource like that. They asked if it was possible to buy them and where they could get those 2000 profiles. I said, "I'm so glad you asked. I brought them with me. They are not for sale but we will give them to you freely, just be sure to credit my friend and me as the authors of this material.

On one of my visits to another mission organization the young man said it was amazing material that needed to get out where missionaries could access it. He suggested putting the profiles on the Internet. Of course I was familiar with the Internet because I was doing it on the website for the C&MA, but I didn't know how to upload a database of this size. He said he could take these 2000 profiles and get them organized, indexed and placed on the Internet making them available to everyone.

I gave him the 2000 profiles and within 24 hours he had it ready. He put it on a website and I linked it to our Christian and Missionary Alliance website. What a wonderful privilege that was to be involved in reaching the unreached with all these profiles.

That is not the end of this story. We were serving as pastor in a very difficult community for five years. I was under a great deal of stress, so much so that I wanted to quit ministry. I prayed and told the Lord I needed to take a year off. I needed a sabbatical. I needed to go away for a year or even two years to get rested up. I was so burned out I even hated to look at churches when we travelled. I began to pray for the Lord to find a way for me to get out of pastoral ministry. I told the Lord I was willing to work a secular job, I'd even drive a school bus, but I needed rest.

About that time I got a phone call from the national office of the Christian and Missionary Alliance. They had been aware of my unofficial Alliance website. It had a lot of information and many people were finding it a rich resource of information about the Christian and Missionary Alliance. They had received a phone call from someone who had been on my website and wanted to make a donation to the Christian and Missionary Alliance. They made a sizable donation to the denomination. Our headquarters was calling me to tell me they were going to be starting the denomination's own website and they wanted to know if I would consider being their webmaster. They asked me to come to Colorado Springs and interview for this job.

All of this was a shock to me because I'm not a trained webmaster. I was self taught. Everything I knew about computers I learned by the seat of my pants. I studied computer programming and learned basic programming on my own. I even had my own newsletter that was circulated in the United States and in Britain for the particular computer that I was using. I was a self-taught person and competing for this job against IT professionals, guys that were trained to do this kind of work.

We went to Colorado Springs to have an interview for the job of webmaster. We had our lengthy interview with the director of communications. The president of the Christian Missionary Alliance came in and sat with me and talked to me about the unreached people groups and about the website, what I might do and how I could help them with this project. In the end I was offered the job. However, they offered me about $10,000 less than I was making in my ministry. I told him what I was making and that I wasn't willing to earn less, but if they could match my income I would consider being the webmaster. The boss talked about it, looked at his figures, and came back to me and said, "We will do it. We will match your current salary if you would come and be our webmaster."

I was thrilled. For me it was a miracle that they offered me. This job was an answer to my prayer. It got me out of pastoral ministries for the two years that I would spend at Colorado Springs. It was yet another way God provided for me in a time of great need. He was restoring me.

He Sends Refreshing
Acts 16:9
*And a vision appeared to Paul in the night;
There was a man of Macedonia standing, beseeching him,
and saying, Come over into Macedonia, and help us.*

While we were at the national office God was doing something else in my heart and life. I have mentioned that I was discouraged and burned out from a stressful pastorate. One of the things we longed to do in Colorado Springs was to attend an exciting church that was very meaningful to us. We had visited there on several occasions when we traveled to visit Colorado Springs. This was a church that was a phenomenal missions church, a charismatic church, and a church where you could sense the presence of God. Every time we went to their services the worship was just awesome. It was a time of refreshing and intimate fellowship with the Lord. It was also a time when God was touching our hearts, melting, molding and changing us in ways that we desperately needed.

I remember one Sunday morning we were standing worshiping the Lord lifting our hands in praise. There was passionate worship going on all across the congregation. There were probably 3,000 people gathered together in that service and that was only one of two services.

As we stood worshiping the presence of the Lord was so real we were weeping. It seemed that in every service we ended up weeping because the presence of God was so powerful and the message was so directed at our hearts.

As I stood there worshiping the Lord I looked around at the crowd and said to the Lord, "Why can't I have a church like this? This is what Alliance churches used to be like. Why can't I have an Alliance church that's on fire for God? Why can't I be used in a place where people are hungry for the word of God?"

The Lord whispered to my heart, "Look around you." I looked around and saw people of every walk of life, rich people, poor people, black people, white people, Hispanic people, and Asian people. They were raising their hands and voices in loud praise to the Lord. Some of them were even on their faces on the floor worshiping the Lord for the awesomeness of his presence.

The Lord said, "Look at these people. They love me more than anything in the world. They don't really care what anybody else thinks about them. They're not showing off with their hands raised. They're not concerned about somebody judging them. They are just here to worship me. They love me more than they love anything else in this world." I responded, "Lord, I love you too. I love you more than anything in this world."

Then the Lord said something that stopped me in my tracks. He said, "No you don't. You don't love me more than anything in this world. You love your ministry more than you love me."

Wow! That was an amazing revelation to my heart. And it was true. I loved preaching. I loved teaching. I loved doing what I was doing on the website. I loved training people for ministry. I loved missions. But the Lord said, "You don't love me as much as you love those things." Then the Lord said, "If you want to pastor a church like this you have to change the way you do your ministry. You have to love me more than you love your ministry. If you go back into pastoral ministries you have to prioritize your love for me and your time with me more than anything else in the world. I no longer want you to worry about the attendance or building a strong church. I want you to work on being a man of God. I want you to be a man of my presence. I want you to love me more than you love your ministry."

That began a new adventure for me. The Lord was more important than my success in ministry. God was more important than the growth of any church.

From there God called us back into pastoral ministry in Pennsylvania where the Spirit of God was poured out on the congregation and we witnessed powerful miracles and phenomenal growth through the presence of God in that place. But that's another story that I've shared in my book titled, *Shekinah Glory*. I hope you will read it and rejoice in the demonstration of the power and presence of God in an average church.

Other Books by Richard W. LaFountain

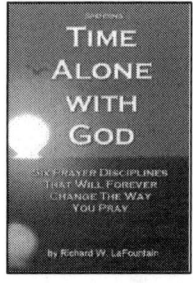

"*Spending Time Alone With God*" is the first of Pastor Dick's books on prayer and intimacy with God. It's the story of his own struggle to pray and stay in the presence of God without getting bored and sleepy. God led him to a prayer pattern that has been effective in his own prayer journey and has proved useful to many others over the last 25 years. Now it is available to you too. It's more than a book. It's more like a training manual with disciplines to work at in your own prayer life. It will transform the way your pray!

"*3-Minutes Alone with God*" is a follow-up to "*Spending Time Alone with God.*" This book gives you helps and tools for your prayer life that will make praying more enjoyable and exciting. Included in this book is a workbook to help you develop prayer skills. The workbook portion is also available online in an 8 ½ x 11 format, ideal for printing your own copies. It is free of charge.

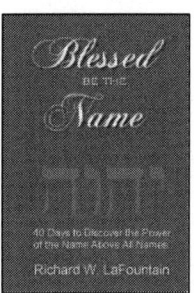

Blessed be the Name
A 40-Day Devotional on Old Testament Names of God

Dick takes you on a walk through some of the names of the Lord in the Old Testament. God has given us over 700 Names of the Lord in Scripture so that we might know and experience God in all his love and glory. It's a great study for the Advent Season. Each chapter contains questions for discussion.

No Sweeter Name
A 40-Day Devotional on New Testament Names of God

Pastor Dick takes you on a walk through some of the names of Jesus in the New Testament. Both Old and New Testament are filled with names, descriptions, and titles of the Lord that help us to appreciate who the Lord Jesus is and wants to be in our daily lives. It's a great study for the Advent Season. Each chapter contains questions for discussion. . .

These books and other prayer products are available only at www.PrayerToday.org and www.MinistryToday.org.

Restoring Shattered Faith
"When your world falls apart and God doesn't save the day."

While serving as missionaries in Brazil in 1982 Dick's daughter was struck by a car and died. He shares that experience and the subsequent discouragement and depression which left his faith shattered and almost lost. He guides us through the story of hurt and healing and the path to restoring shattered faith.

The Shekinah Glory
When God's glory invades the church.

This book tells the story of a 21st century church that experienced that manifest presence of God in a dramatic way. This mysterious presence of God has hovered over the congregation for nearly a decade. It proves to us that God is indeed still on the throne, his hand is not shortened that he cannot save, heal, deliver and manifest His glorious presence among us. He is the same yesterday, today and forever.

These books are only available online at

www.PrayerToday.org
and
www.MinistryToday.org

or you can request a copy by writing to Pastor Dick LaFountain at

PastorDickLaf@gmail.com